Richard Peace

OBLOMOV

A Critical Examination of Goncharov's Novel

BIRMINGHAM SLAVONIC MONOGRAPHS NO.20

Richard Peace

Oblomov

A Critical Examination of Goncharov's Novel

Published by the   Department of Russian Language and Literature
University of Birmingham
P.O. Box 363
Birmingham B15 2TT

© Series: University of Birmingham
© Contents No. 20 : Richard Peace

ISBN   0 7044 1161 X
ISSN   0141-3805

FOOTNOTES

All references to the text of *Oblomov* are to the *Literaturnyi pamyatnik* edition: I.A. Goncharov, *Oblomov, Roman v chetyrekh chastyakh*, izdanie podgotovila L.S. Geiro, Leningrad, "Nauka", Leningradskoe otdelenie, 1987. This excellent edition establishes the canonical text, gives variants and supplies commentary and notes. Page references to this edition are given in brackets. Other references to this edition are preceded by the contraction *L.P.*

M. = Moscow   L. = Leningrad

CONTENTS

Introduction

Goncharov's novel *Oblomov* occupies a unique place in the history of Russian culture. It is the only one of his works which is an undoubted masterpiece, and it has preserved its reputation and its contemporary relevance, not only because it points to phenomena that lie deep within the Russian national consciousness, but also because of what it reveals of the human psyche at large. Turgenev, whom Goncharov saw as his rival, perceived the national significance of the novel, and said to its author: *'Oblomov* will be remembered as long as there is still one Russian left alive.'[1]   Dostoyevsky spoke of Goncharov's 'great mind', and in a humorous piece of 1886 Chekhov placed Goncharov, along with Tolstoy, as the two living figures highest in a 'Literary Table of Ranks'.[2] Although he was later to revise this view, the influence of *Oblomov* can be found throughout Chekhov's works.

The novel is a *tour de force.*   Goncharov has taken what is apparently the most intractable of themes – the indolence and inactivity of a lethargic man – and created a great comic novel, which at the same time is full of deep pathos and psychological insight. Moreover, the novel seems modern in many ways: its exploration of childhood as a key to the psychological problems of the adult; and its almost 'feminist' analysis of the problems of a woman in marriage, for example. Indeed, in 1883, when a delegation of Russian women visited Goncharov as a mark of respect for fifty years of literary activity, they particularly praised him for his portrayal of women.[3]

Yet it was as a parable reflecting the problems of Russian society itself that the novel received its greatest critical acclaim in the influential article 'What is Oblomovism?' by the chief radical critic of the time, N.A. Dobrolyubov. Its arguments may strike the modern reader as forced, but they delighted Goncharov himself and the social interpretation of the novel has had a tenacious life of its own. A later son of Goncharov's own Simbirsk Province, V.I. Lenin, pressed the novel into service in his fight against bureaucratic inefficiency:

> There was a certain typical figure of Russian life, Oblomov. He lay on his bed all the time and made plans. A great deal of time has passed since then. Russia has had three revolutions, and still the Oblomovs have remained; for Oblomov was not only a

---

[1] Quoted in I.S. Geiro, 'Roman I.A. Goncharova *Oblomov* ', *L.P.*, 547.

[2] See Geiro, *L.P.*, 549; and A.P. Chekhov, *Polnoe sobranie sochinenii i pisem v tridsati tomakh*, M., 1974-83, Vol. 5, 143 (the piece first appeared in *Oskolki*, 1886).

[3] See Geiro, *L.P.*, 547-8.

landowner, but a peasant, not only a peasant, but a member of the intelligentsia, not only a member of the intelligentsia, but a worker and a communist. One has only to look at us, at how we have our meetings, how we work in the commissions in order to say that *the old Oblomov remains and we have to wash him, clean him, shove and push him a long time in order for any sense at all to come out of him.* On account of this we must look at our position without any illusions.[4]

That Lenin should interpret the figure of Oblomov in this way is not so surprising – he made frequent use of the classics of Russian literature for polemical ends – but what is more remarkable is that this quotation, with its italicised message, should be pressed into political service in a much more recent article, which seeks to show the figure of Oblomov as emblematic of the period of stagnation under Brezhnev, and clearly suggests the relevance of Shtol'ts for the new entrepreneurial policy of *perestroika* (not, it might be added, without overtones of a more pessimistic view of the nature of Russian man himself). The article's conclusion is quite clear about the relevance of Goncharov's novel for contemporary Soviet society:

> *Oblomov* was a harsh warning to a culture, [a warning] which contemporaries did not recognise, ascribing the problems of the novel to a former age, or to one that was already passing. It required a hundred years to elapse, it required living through a revolution, a civil war, the Stalin terror, decades of stagnation and inactivity, in order for the culturally significant actuality of a great novel to become apparent.[5]

It is not without significance that Mikhail Gorbachev himself has talked of 'Oblomovs' in characterising those who are slow to implement his policy of *perestroika,* and the relevance of *Oblomov* for contemporary Soviet society was pointed up in a film version, shot mostly in present-day Moscow, and shown on British television in 1990. The American actor George Wendt was an English-speaking Oblomov, whom the film presented as a typical Soviet politician, lobbied by a succession of Russian-speaking Muscovites on the need for action, but who, in typical Oblomov fashion, preferred the comforts of his own sybaritic life to the upset and strain of pursuing active policies. The contemporary political point of this version of *Oblomov* is only too sharp and clear.

---

[4] Quoted in V. Kantor, 'Dolgii navyk k snu' (Razmyshleniya o romane I.A. Goncharova *Oblomov*), *Voprosy literatury*, No. 1, 1989, 163.
[5] *Ibid.*, 183.

Yet the novel has significance beyond that of its continuing relevance for Russian society and Russian culture. Happy, indeed, would be the reader, who behind laughter at Oblomov's subterfuges and inconsistencies, behind exasperation at his fecklessness and inadequacy, would not be aware, too, of an uneasy feeling of self-recognition.

4

Chapter I

Genesis and Form

The first part of the novel to be written was the section entitled 'The Dream of Oblomov'. Goncharov finished this in October of 1848, and it was printed as a separate piece, under the title 'An Episode from an Unfinished Novel', in March 1849 in an anthology with illustrations brought out by the journal *The Contemporary*. At this point, however, a kind of 'Oblomovism' appears to have affected the author; for although he claimed to be working on the novel itself, it was a further ten years before it saw publication, and yet the writing of the bulk of the novel was accomplished in one of those rare spurts of activity of which Oblomov himself was capable.[1]

In the summer of 1857 Goncharov was staying in Marienbad, and as he records: 'I came here on the 21st of June old style, and today the 29th of July I have the first part of *Oblomov* complete, all the second part has been written and a good deal of the third, so that the wood is already thinning, and in the distance I can see... the end.'[2] During that summer in Marienbad it was as though the novel were being dictated to him by someone: words flowed effortlessly from his pen as they did for his hero Oblomov when he fell under the spell of Olga Ilinskaya. Indeed for author and hero alike such unwonted activity appeared to have a common inspiration. Thus Goncharov wrote to a correspondent:

> Know that I am preoccupied... and you will not be mistaken if you say with a woman. Yes, with a woman. It does not matter that I am forty-five, I am greatly preoccupied with Olga Ilinskaya (...) I can scarcely bear to drink my three beakers [of spa water (R.A.P.)] and run round the whole of Marienbad from six o'clock to nine o'clock hardly having time to drink tea on the way, before I take a cigar and go straight to her. I sit in her room, or I go to the park and take myself off into the most lonely walks.[3]

The novel finally appeared in print in 1859, serialised in *Fatherland Notes* from January to April, but not before it had undergone some last-minute revision. Thus the series of St Petersburg types who visit

---

[1] See Milton Ehre, *Oblomov and his Creator : The Life and Art of Ivan Goncharov*, Princeton, New Jersey, 1973, 88-90.
[2] Letter to Yu. D. Yefremova, Marienbad, 29 July/9 August 1857, I .A. Goncharov, *Sobranie sochinenii v vos'mi tomakh*, M., 1952-5, Vol. 8, 285.
[3] Letter to I.I. L'khovskii, Marienbad, 15/17 July 1857, *ibid.*, 281-2.

Oblomov at the beginning of Part I was added only before going to press. [4]

The way in which the novel was written has left its mark on the form. The interrupted nature of the writing has its parallel in certain narrative dislocations. Thus Part I starts on a comic note – almost, indeed, like a Molière comedy – with a central character who exhibits a stock vice (laziness) from which the comedy itself flows, channelled through the well-established comedic tradition of the relationship between master and servant. There then follows a section of visits to Oblomov by a succession of figures representing quintessential 'types' to be found in the capital city. These five visits seem an obvious echo of Gogol's masterpiece *Dead Souls* and the visits paid by Chichikov to five typical representatives of Russian provincial life. But Goncharov has inverted the Gogolian device of the 'portrait gallery': not only are they types of the capital city rather than the provinces, but whereas Gogol's *Poema* is based on travel, Goncharov's novel is predicated on inertia, so that, given Oblomov's laziness, these St Petersburg types have to visit him.

There then follows 'The Dream of Oblomov', which represents a dislocation on more than one level. Its function in the narrative is that of a 'flashback' to Oblomov's childhood, and at the same time it represents a kernel of great thematic and psychological importance for the novel itself. Yet, as we have seen, the dream was published ten years earlier and in a context which seemed to place it as a study in the spirit of the 'Natural School' of the 1840s – a sketch depicting a way of life: the mores and values of the rural gentry. The date of its original publication is also significant; 1849 marked a period of political clamp-down after the European revolutions of 1848. It was the year in which Dostoyevsky was arrested for publicly reading Belinsky's famous letter to Gogol. The prevailing atmosphere of the 'Dream', with its stagnation and prohibition on youthful activity, seemed to catch the mood of the time, yet this apparent period piece of the late 1840s has been injected into a novel set in the post-Crimean War period of the Great Reforms, a period of political upsurge and hope in Russian life. At this level the temporal dislocation once again mirrors the theme of long stagnation and sudden activity.

The idyll presented by the dream is a different genre from the comedy which has gone before, yet once again the influence of Gogol can be detected. Like Gogol's 'Old-World Landowners' the dream depicts an old-fashioned way of life described in a way which hovers between nostalgic approval and implied criticism. Gogol's idyllic world is lost through its lack of descendants – it is a world lacking in children, but Goncharov places a child and his observing eye at the very centre of his ambivalent idyll, and it is this which carries the lost idyll into the present.

---

[4] L.S. Geiro, 'Istoriya sozdaniya i publikatsii romana *Oblomov* ', *L.P.*, 593, and A.F. Zakharkin, *Roman I.A. Goncharova Oblomov*, M., 1963, 83.

The dream is interrupted by the arrival of Shtol'ts, who in Part II forces his friend out into society. Yet this new, enforced activity of Oblomov is given no tangible depiction in the novel, we are only presented with its results in the form of Oblomov's criticisms of the life he has experienced. A further dislocation occurs when Oblomov leaves his St Petersburg apartment for a *dacha* and life in the country on the outskirts of the capital. Oblomov is already well acquainted with Olga, and Zakhar is now married. The reader is thus presented with the changes in Oblomov's life, before their explanation. Such inversion of the event and its result is noticeable in the further development of the emotional life of the central characters. In Part IV Chapter 4 the reader is given a further flashback to the time when Shtol'ts himself becomes interested in Olga. Indeed only in Chapter 4 does he disclose that he is now married to her. At the end of the novel Oblomov's marriage to Agafya Matveyevna is similarly disclosed as a *fait accompli* but not before the reader has been made aware of the enigmatic presence of a new child in the household.

Such narrational procedures, it may be argued, show a preoccupation with states rather than actions, a preoccupation entirely consonant with the subject matter of the novel. Indeed on the final page the novel itself is presented to the reader as the explanation of a state. A *litterateur* (a thinly disguised authorial self-portrait) is walking in St Petersburg with Shtol'ts, and expresses the wish to know how beggars come about – *otkuda berutsya nishchie*? The beggar chosen for cross-questioning turns out to be Zakhar, and the explanation of his *state* is given by Shtol'ts as arising from another *state*: 'Oblomovism'. When the *litterateur* seeks an explanation of this strange term Shtol'ts complies by asking him to write down all he is about to tell him; the novel ends with the words: 'and he told him all that is written down here'. This is the final narrative dislocation: a novel (which in more than one sense can be seen to have developed chronologically from the embryo of Oblomov's dream), we are now led to believe, actually sprang from its ending.

This sudden inversion is not only striking in formal terms, it also strongly suggests a social interpretation of all that has gone before.

Chapter II

Oblomovism and Russian Society

The novel, therefore, has come about as an explanation of the term *Oblomovism,* which in itself is suggested as an answer to the question: 'where do beggars come from?' Zakhar, the concrete focus of this enquiry, explains his condition in terms of the changing times. The gentry no longer need the servants they had in the old days – now they take off their own boots: the gentry is in decline, and servants nowadays have to be literate. This is very much an ending in the spirit of the post-Crimean War period of reform, when great changes were afoot, and not only in education. By 1859 moves to emancipate the serfs from their masters were already well advanced, and when the reform itself came in 1861, it would indeed herald the decline of the gentry as a class, not, of course, in the way Zakhar sees the decline; for the irony of his explanation is that it champions the very values of Oblomovism which Shtol'ts sees as the root cause of the problem. The gentry were proving incapable of forsaking their old indolent ways for the new economic values represented by Shtol'ts himself.

Given this authorial lead it is not surprising that Dobrolyubov's famous article on the novel should devote itself to the problem of *Oblomovism* interpreted in strictly social terms.[1] Goncharov himself approved of Dobrolyubov's article and said so to his friends. Thus he wrote to the memoirist Annenkov:

> After this article, if another critic is not to repeat it, it only remains for him to indulge in reproaches, or leaving the question of *Oblomovism* on one side to speak about the female characters.[2]

Nevertheless, unlike Dobrolyubov's article, Goncharov's novel is anything but a social or political tract. The work is far too complex, its social statements far too ambivalent, and the modern reader may well have difficulty in reconciling Dobrolyubov's arguments with the novel he has just read. Yet the social theme is strongly present in the novel, and not just in the negative sense which the ending appears to affirm, and which was developed in more general terms by Dobrolyubov.

Oblomov and Shtol'ts are clearly antithetical figures. The author speculates on how they could be friends, when, in the case of Oblomov:

---

[1] See N.A. Dobrolyubov, 'Chto takoe Oblomovshchina?' *Sobranie sochinenii v devyati tomakh,* M.-L., 1961-4, Vol. 4, 307-44. 'Oblomovism' (*Oblomovshchina*) was Goncharov's original title for his novel. See Geiro, *L.P.,* 554.
[2] See letter to P.V. Annenkov, 20 May 1859 (also letter to I.I. L'khovskii of same date), Goncharov, *Sob. soch.,* Vol. 8, 320, 323.

'Every trait, every step, his whole existence was a blatant protest against the life led by Shtol'ts'. (130) Shtol'ts is 'Western man' – he is a Russian (or half-Russian) with a German name. He is a man of affairs, a man of action, yet it is one of the novel's weaknesses that he is scarcely credible as a figure. For one thing we never enter the active world of this man of action, we are not presented with the reality of any of his practical undertakings.[3] In the figure of Shtol'ts practicality is presented as a state, just as much as is Oblomov's inertia, it is not practicality on the wing.

Apart from what might be a congenital inability to deal with characterisation other than as a 'state', Goncharov had another problem to face in his depiction of Shtol'ts – such men did not as yet exist in Russia:

> In order for such a character to be formed, perhaps such mixed elements are necessary as those which formed Shtol'ts. For a long time men of action in Russia have been poured into five or six stereotyped moulds. Lazily, looking around them with eyes half shut, they have set their hands to the engine of society, and drowsily moved it along its accustomed rut, placing their feet in the tracks left by their predecessors. But now eyes have opened after sleep, sprightly, bold footsteps can be heard, lively voices...How many Shtoltses are destined to appear with Russian names! (130)[4]

The type of Shtol'ts is, therefore, more a hope for the future than a present reality. Yet Goncharov was not alone in his difficulties with portraying such figures. Gogol before him had attempted to depict the positive entrepreneur in Part II of *Dead Souls,* but his Kostanzhoglo (who is also of mixed racial origin) is no more convincing.

The problem was the nature of Russian society itself. In the nineteenth century the prosperity of Western Europe, particularly of such countries as Britain and France, was founded on the rise of an affluent middle class and such 'captains of industry' as mill-owners, ironmasters and colonial traders. They were the dynamic force behind western society and their profiles are faithfully drawn in the Western European novel in figures such as Charles Dickens's Dombey and Balzac's César Birotteau. One looked in vain for these types in Russia; here society was polarised between those with rank and those without. The Russian merchant might, on the face of it, seem to supply the

---

[3] Geiro sees hints at Shtol'ts's commercial activity in the list of Russian towns he visits. *L.P.,* 534.

[4] The Magarshack translation of *deyateli* ('men of action') as 'statesmen' is inaccurate and not consonant with censorship restrictions of the time. See Ivan Goncharov, *Oblomov,* translated and with an Introduction by David Magarshack, Harmondsworth, 1959, 164.

missing middle class, but nothing could be further from the truth. The merchants, although often wealthy, were traditionalists and arch-conservatives, whose values were nearer to those of Oblomov than Shtol'ts. Such industry as existed was being developed often by foreign, rather than Russian, entrepreneurs. Goncharov himself came from a merchant milieu and was educated at a commercial school; he could see the problem more clearly than most. His portrayal of Shtol'ts is a brave attempt to supply Russia's missing entrepreneurial class: men of action who in the future, and with fully Russian names, would rouse the country from its torpor. As yet, this was merely a promise rather than a living reality, and Goncharov realised his failure with the portrayal of Shtol'ts: 'He is weak, pale, the idea can be seen too nakedly in him.' [5]

The figure of Oblomov is far more complex, far more rounded, nevertheless it also contains the element of an 'idea'. It is not merely that the quality associated with him has taken on abstract and general significance in the term *Oblomovism*; for long before Shtol'ts coined it in Part II, Oblomov has already been projected as a figure of general, as well as of particular, significance. In his first exchange with Zakhar over the latter's reluctance to clean his room, we are told that his master seemed to think: 'Well, brother, you're still more of an Oblomov than I am myself'. (13) The name, then, is not just his own, it has some general, some symbolic significance.

Later Oblomov complains about his wasted talents: 'For twelve years a light has been locked up within me which has been seeking for an outlet, yet it has only burned its prison, it has not torn itself free but has faded away.'(145)   Shtol'ts recommends him to settle with his peasants either on the banks of the Volga or in Siberia, and Oblomov retorts: 'Am I alone? Just look: Mikhailov, Petrov, Semenov, [Alekseyev], Stepanov...You cannot count them all: our name is legion. '(145)[6]

Such a statement seems to cast Oblomov as the quintessential 'superfluous man' – a point boldly developed by Dobrolyubov.

Nevertheless, the symbolism surrounding Oblomov is more subtle and more wide-ranging than that. If in the portrayal of Shtol'ts Western

---

[5] i.e. in *Luchshe pozdno, chem nikogda.* See Goncharov, *Sob. soch.,* Vol. 8, 80. Setchkarev contests the view of Shtol'ts as a mere social stereotype: 'So many relevant details of Shtol'ts's charachter have gone unnoticed, obscured by dogmatic views of him.'   See Vsevolod Setchkarev, *Ivan Goncharov: His Life and Works*, Würzburg, 1974, 151   (See also 140, 147).

Nevertheless, Goncharov himself was fond of such social and cultural antitheses. He ends the first chapter of *Fregat Pallada* with contrasting descriptions of the lives of the typical English gentleman and his Russian counterpart, and concludes: 'We have become so rooted to home, that wherever and no matter how long I were to travel, I would carry away the soil of my native Oblomovka on my feet everywhere I went, and no oceans could wash it away! ' Goncharov, *Sob. soch.,* Vol. 2, 73.

[6] In his definitive version, Goncharov removed the name of Alekseyev from this list (*L.P.,* 145, 626).

values are stressed, the presentation of Oblomov from the outset has clear overtones of the East. His *khalat* (dressing gown), the recurrent motif of his *Oblomovism*, is described as being of 'Persian material', a real eastern *khalat* 'without the slightest hint of Europe'; its sleeves are cut 'according to the unalterable Asiatic fashion'[7] and it has two other features which suggest qualities of Asiatic Russia: it is enormously broad, and is like a slave in its submissiveness to Oblomov's movements. Moreover we are also told that Oblomov's estates are located so deep in the provinces that they are almost in Asia (46) and that Zakhar treats his master in the rude and familiar way in which an Asiatic witch doctor (*shaman*) treats his idol. (59)

Thus in the relationship between Shtol'ts and Oblomov we appear to have a confrontation between the values of the West and the values of the East; the pull between a conservative nostalgia for the life of old semi-Asiatic Russia and the attractions of progress as represented in the entrepreneurial values of the West. It is a pull between two poles of attraction which goes to the very heart of Russian self-questioning in the nineteenth century – a divided consciousness, symbolically expressed in the national emblem of the two-headed eagle, looking in two different directions at once. In intellectual terms this cleavage in the national consciousness found expression in the debates between the Slavophiles and the Westernisers – two opposing camps, many of whose members, like Oblomov and Shtol'ts themselves, had actually been friends in their youth.

The Slavophiles took to wearing Russian 'national' clothing, which, as in the case of Oblomov's *khalat*, was an outward sign of their inner orientation. *Khalat* is usually translated as 'dressing gown', and therefore to that extent it points to Oblomov's inability fully to face the waking world.

Nevertheless Oblomov himself corrects Volkov when the latter calls it a dressing gown (*shlafrok*): 'It is not a *shlafrok*', he says, 'it is a *khalat*' (*eto ne shlafrok, a khalat*).(17) In effect the *khalat* is an old-fashioned item of Russian apparel. Pushkin had already used it as an element of characterisation in *Eugene Onegin* to symbolise the quaint old-fashioned ways of Tatyana's father,[8] and in the language itself the phrase *khalatnaya zhizn'* ('life lived in a *khalat*') is often used to indicate an easy-going attitude to life.

---

7 The Magarshack translation blurs this distinction: 'It's a perfectly good dressing gown'. Magarshack, 25.

8 Cf. A.S. Pushkin, *Yevgenii Onegin*, Ch. ii, v. 34 ('*A sam v khalate el i pil*'). In his reminiscences 'Back Home' (*Na rodine*) Goncharov describes a neighbouring landowner, Kozyrev, who never 'got out of his *khalat*" (*On ne vykhodil iz khalata*). When he and another neighbour came to town they would stay wth Goncharov's godfather, and all three would lie in bed all day, merely getting up briefly for lunch. Goncharov concludes that as a child this way of life must have impressed itself on his observant mind, and given rise to his ideas about *Oblomovism*. See Goncharov, *Sob. soch.*, Vol. 7, 241-2.

Oblomov's *khalat* may be 'Asiatic' but it is still very Russian, and for all that its material is 'Persian', it is perhaps worth bearing in mind the scathing remark of Chaadayev that when the Slavophile Konstantin Aksakov wore his 'Russian' costume, the peasants mistook him for a Persian.[9]

Oblomov is not just a lazy man, he has pretensions to be a philosopher. It is Shtol'ts who identifies him as such on hearing the outline of Oblomov's vision of the ideal life (138). Yet these ideals lie in the old Russian way of life, such as it was on his family estate of Oblomovka, and the actual chronology of composition – as we have seen – links his dream-return to Oblomovka with the period of the 1840s. Moreover, Oblomov's discovery that 'the horizon of his activity and daily existence lay within himself'(53) seems further to identify him with the inward-looking 'life of the spirit' (*zhizn' v dukhe*) so typical of the 'men of the forties', as also does his youthful passion for poetry (52). By contrast Shtol'ts is a 'man of the sixties'. Towards the end of the novel Oblomov is described as a Russian Plato, who has been preordained 'to express the possibility of the ideally quiet side of human existence' (368). The identification with Plato is again suggestive. The philosophy is that of an ideal whose lineaments can only vaguely be perceived in the shadowy imperfection of human life, and it is this gulf between ideal and reality which is expressed through Oblomov's repeated cry *'Kogda zhe zhit'?'* (52) ('When can one begin to live?')

Yet the polarisation of values presented through Oblomov and Shtol'ts is not quite as schematic as it might seem. The pull between East and West is going on within Oblomov himself. The anomaly of his position is that this denizen of the Russian Asiatic hinterland is actually, throughout the whole course of the novel, living in the most westward-looking city in Russia – the capital, St Petersburg. Despite the fact that there is both economic and emotional pressure on him to return to his roots, to revisit the Oblomovka which so enthralls him in his dream, he successfully resists it, even though (and, of course, it might even be argued, because) his marriage to Olga depends on this. Nevertheless he is not happy in St Petersburg, and only appears to come into his own in a rural setting, be it the countryside outside the capital where he hires a *dacha*, or the re-creation of Oblomovka in the house of Agafya Matveyevna on the Vyborg side of the river.

Oblomov is a man divided; his lethargy is conditioned by two opposing 'dreams'. One evokes his childhood in Oblomovka, and orientates him towards an idealised and untroubled past; the other is a daydream – the constant turning over in his mind of his 'plan' for reforming his estate along western lines. From the opening pages we are

---

[9] See A. Walicki, *The Slavophile Controversy: History of a Conservative Utopia in Nineteenth Century Russian Thought* (trans. Hilda Andrews-Rusiecka), Oxford, 1975, 238. For Goncharov's own view on Asiatic influence still observable in Russian life see *Fregat Pallada*, Goncharov, *Sob. soch.*, Vol. 3, 180.

made aware that Oblomov is not just lying on his couch, he is formulating his plan: 'According to this plan it was proposed to introduce various new measures, economic, and also to do with policing as well as other matters.'(10) This plan is to affect his whole life and will be consonant with the new times: 'From this a large part of the pattern of life which he sketched in his solitude was occupied with a plan, new and fresh and consonant with the demands of the time – a plan for organising his estate and governing his peasants.' (53) Needless to say this 'plan' only exists as a dream in his mind. It is not backed up by any concrete detail which might enable it to be put into practice, nor is it even put down on paper.

There is a sense in which Oblomov, like Russia itself, is being pulled in two directions at once. On the one hand there are the patriarchal blandishments of the past, represented by Oblomovka and Agafya Matveyevna – on the other the active 'Western' values of Shtol'ts and Olga. Both Shtol'ts and Olga seem bent on resurrecting Oblomov, concerned to awaken him from his sleep like the reformers of the post-Crimean War period, hauling Russia itself from the stagnation of the regime of Nicholas I, symbolised by the 'Dream' first published during his reign. It is as though, in the novel, the values of 1859 are confronting those of 1849.

In 'The Dream of Oblomov' the difference between 'new' and 'old' attitudes is posited in geographical terms:

> ... and just as in another place the bodies of people were rapidly burned out from the volcanic workings of an inner spiritual fire, so the souls of the inhabitants of Oblomovka foundered peacefully, and without hindrance in their soft bodies. (96-97)

Oblomov himself is now in 'another place', St Petersburg, and his inner life has the new potential of 'spiritual fire': the volcanic workings of a fiery head and a humanitarian heart'.(56) Oblomov's humanitarian heart reveals values close to the new denunciatory mood of social protest which characterised the 1860s.

> It would also happen that he would become full of contempt for human vice, falsehood and slander, for the evil that flooded the world, and he would burn with a desire to show a man his vile blemishes, and suddenly his thoughts would be set alight, they would go wandering to and fro in his head like waves in the sea. Then intentions would develop; they would set all his blood on fire, his muscles would begin to twitch, his sinews tighten. Intentions would turn into strong impulses, and moved by a moral force, he would quickly adopt two or three different poses a minute. With blazing eyes he would half raise himself on his bed, would stretch out his hand and look around in inspired fashion...

at any moment his impulse would be realised, it would turn into a mighty deed (*podvig*)... and then, gentlemen! What miracles, what benign consequences one might expect from such a lofty effort! (54)

Thus we see how difficult it is in practice for the 'volcanic fire' to overcome the habits of the 'soft body'.

Oblomov himself feels within him the presence of a rich vein of ore:

At the same time he had the morbid feeling that buried in him as though in a grave there was some kind of good, beneficent principle, which perhaps had already died, or was lying like gold in the depths of a mountain, and that it was already high time that this gold was put into currency. (77)

Among outsiders only Shtol'ts knows of this other side of Oblomov, and towards the end of the novel he claims that he has communicated this view to Olga: 'I brought you to understand that there is in him a mind which is not the inferior of others, only it is buried and squashed by all sorts of rubbish, and from idleness it has fallen asleep.' (362) Shtol'ts identifies the 'gold' as Oblomov's heart, and tells Olga that she loves him: 'because, more precious than any mind, he has an honest and faithful heart! This is his native gold and he has carried it through life unscathed.' (362)[10]

There is a hint of the great power, that could suddenly stir from lethargy, in Oblomov's very name. He is 'Ilya son of Ilya' (Il'ya Il'ich) – a name suggestive of that other Ilya, the titanic figure of Russian folklore, Ilya Muromets (a Russian Achilles or Ulysses (93)) whose deeds he learns about from his nurse. Ilya Muromets remained sitting, apparently paralysed, for 33 years (the age of Oblomov himself at the novel's opening) but when he arose from stasis he performed incredible feats of strength. The figure of Ilya Muromets has been seen as symbolising Russia herself, epitomising her irregular historical development, with its long periods of stagnation and sudden spurts of revolutionary activity.[11] Nevertheless, as we see from the passage quoted earlier, Oblomov can never quite rise from his couch to '*podvig*' and 'miracles' .

---

[10] Oblomov's 'buried gold' may well have had a symbolic echo in the gold prospecting activities of Shtol'ts, which figures in variants of the novel (*L.P.*, 493). In the canonical text Shtol'ts takes Oblomov to dine with a gold prospector (*L.P.*, 136). See also Geiro, *L.P.*, 533.

[11] 'The fact is that in the idealised figure of Il'ya Muromets was fully expressed the historical character of the Russian people.' See entry under 'Il'ya Muromets' in F.A. Brokgauz and I.A. Efron (eds), *Entsiklopedicheskii slovar* ', St Petersburg, 1895, Vol. 24, 949. See also V.I. Mel'nik, *Realizm I.A. Goncharova*, Vladivostok, 1985, 106-7.

The attempt to put Oblomov on his feet, which is undertaken by Shtol'ts and Olga, ends in failure. The dream of Oblomovka has swamped his life – it is even suggested that it is responsible for his stroke at the end of the novel – and now it is impossible to make him whole, as he tells Shtol'ts: 'What do you wish to do with me? I have fallen away forever from that world where you are trying to drag me. You will not fit together the two broken halves...' (374)

If on the level of symbolism, Oblomov seems to take on some of the ontological ambivalence of Russia herself, on a more lowly sociological plane Oblomov can be identified as a symbolic figure with contemporary relevance. When Shtol'ts arrives at the end of Part I and provides a fitting interruption to the idyllic dream of Oblomovka, he tries to make Oblomov face up to his immediate financial problems by actually going back to Oblomovka physically, but Oblomov demurs – his plan is not yet ready, and he scathingly dismisses the various categories of people who need to travel. At this Shtol'ts asks him a fundamental question: 'And who then are you? To which social category do you ascribe yourself?' Oblomov refuses to answer directly, telling Shtol'ts to ask Zakhar. Shtol'ts summons Zakhar from the next room, and asks him who it is who is lying there before him. Zakhar's answer is that it is the master (barin), Ilya Ilich. Shtol'ts is delighted by this answer, it has defined Oblomov socially – he is a barin. When Oblomov himself tries to gloss the term with the English word 'gentleman', Shtol'ts will have none of it: 'A gentleman is the sort of barin...who puts on his socks himself, and himself takes off his boots.' (140) Oblomov, then, is a typical Russian barin, who in contradistinction to his western counterpart has been taught indolence from birth.

This moment is echoed later in the novel in a scene which gives the lie to Oblomov's pretensions to a plan to reform the economy of his estate, when he confesses that he knows nothing about agriculture. Indeed, he is prepared to entrust the management of Oblomovka to such rogues as Ivan Matveyevich and Zatertyi, and when Ivan Matveyevich asks him if he has ever occupied himself with anything, Oblomov gives the meaningful answer that he is a barin: 'Who am I? What am I? Go and ask Zakhar, he will tell you "a barin"! Yes, I am a barin and am not capable of doing anything!' (282) Thus Oblomov accepts Shtol'ts's definition of him, presented here, as earlier, through the eyes of a servant.

Although the concept of barin seems to be treated negatively, it has its appeal to the lower orders, for instance to Zakhar himself, who boasts to his acquaintances that his master is 'a nobleman of lineage' (stolbovoi barin). Part of Oblomov's appeal to Agafya Matveyevna is that he, unlike the other men she knows, is a barin. She contrasts the meek timid behaviour of her former husband with that of Oblomov, whose bold independent glance reveals dominance. (298) Indeed she looks with special favour on the son she has had by Oblomov because he, unlike her other children, is *barchonok* (a nobleman's son) and it is for this reason that she will allow him to be educated by Shtol'ts and Olga.

The values of Agafya Matveyevna, it seems, are not too dissimilar from those of Shtol'ts's own mother, who, we are told: 'dreamed of the ideal of the *barin*, in her son, although he might be an upstart of plebeian blood, from a German-burgher father, he was, all the same, the son of a Russian noblewoman...' (123)   So that, for all that Oblomov and Shtol'ts are presented as opposites (Oblomov – the effete *barin*: Shtol'ts – the bourgeois man of affairs) the latter is not entirely the German burgher that his mother fears he might turn out to be. Her influence as a Russian noblewoman is seen to be beneficial, as is also the civilising effect of the big nobleman's house in Verkhlyovo with its gallery of paintings – not to mention the tempering influence of his contacts with the Oblomov family and Oblomovka.

Shtol'ts's name in German means 'proud', and he has indeed a natural pride – a nobility which comes from his own abilities as a successful man of action. [12] By contrast, Oblomov's pride, as we see throughout the course of the novel, is far more vulnerable. His is not the nobility which stems from action, but from the very static quality of status – he is Oblomov, and that is good enough for him or anyone else. After his first visit by the society man Volkov, Oblomov feels glad that he does not have to take part in the whirl of society and of social events, but can instead lie on his couch preserving his human dignity and his peace. (20)

The question whether *Oblomovism* is an entirely negative condition, or whether it can be seen more positively, as a kind of reflective, quietistic attitude to life, is not entirely resolved in the novel. Among Goncharov's contemporaries, critics such as Dobrolyubov took a negative view, whereas the more conservative Druzhinin saw positive values in Oblomov's attitude to life.[13] Yet, however Oblomov himself might try to present his life at the end of the novel, it is clear that the opening sections of Part I, which project Oblomov as a comic character, soon yield to a more tragic view of the hero, vainly struggling against the burden fate has placed upon him: ' "Why am I like this?" Oblomov asked himself, almost in tears, and again he hid his head under the blanket, "Why indeed?" '(78) Amidst this self-questioning he falls asleep, and the answer to why he is as he is appears

---

[12] Geiro sees a reply to the 'pride' of Shtol'ts in the dove-like tenderness (*golubinaya nezhnost'*) of Oblomov (*L.P.*, 363) and links Shtol'ts's first name, Andrei, to that of the saint Andrei Pervozvannyi ('Andrew the first-called') in as much as Shtol'ts is the pioneer of a new life. In a draft version a prototype of Shtol'ts was called Pochayev, a name which Geiro links to the verb *pochinat'* ('to begin', 'to lay a foundation'), *L.P.*, 535.

[13] A.V. Druzhinin, '*Oblomov*. Roman I.A. Goncharova. Dva toma, Spb., 1895', *Biblioteka dlya chteniya*, 1895, No.12, otd. IV, 1-25.

to be provided by his ensuing dream – the section 'The Dream of Oblomov' which in many respects is the kernel of the whole work.

Chapter III

The Dream

The dream transports Oblomov back to the patriarchal estate of his childhood. It is an idyllic world from which all the dramatic features of a romantic landscape are absent – no mountains, no seas: just the flat Russian plain. In part Goncharov seems indebted to Gogol's idealised view of the Ukraine presented in the opening story of his collection *Evenings in a Village near Dikanka*: 'The sky there, on the contrary, appears to squeeze closer to the earth, but not to throw its bolts with more force, but perhaps only in order to embrace it with love more firmly'. (79)[1] Yet whereas sexual imagery in Gogol's natural description is overt and disturbing, Goncharov goes on to give us a more reassuring explanation for this loving embrace of earth and sky – the love is parental: 'It [the sky] stretched as low overhead, as a trusty, parental roof, in order, so it seemed, to guard this select region from all misfortunes.'(79) Nature is just as watchful over its children, we are to assume, as are Oblomov's parents over their pampered child.

The other literary source for Oblomov's dream is again Gogol. His story *The Old-World Landowners* presents a rural idyll, a vanished way of life, which like the 'Dream' itself hovers ambivalently between nostalgic endorsement and implied criticism. Both are enclosed worlds. The interests of Gogol's old-world landowners are concentrated on themselves in much the same way as are those of the inhabitants of Oblomovka: 'Their interests were concentrated on them themselves, not crossing or touching those of any others'. (83)[2]

Gogol identifies his two old-world landowners in classical terms as Philomen and Baucis. Goncharov, too, makes use of a variety of classical references to suggest this way of life as age-old – a normative world of stasis existing outside time, whose features are calmly classical rather than the turbulent landscapes of romantic art.

At certain times the peasants take their grain to harbours on the Volga, which are the 'Colchis' and 'Pillars of Hercules' of their classical world (83), and somewhere beyond the confines of their microcosm the 'dark world' begins, as it did for the ancients. 'The norm of life was ready-made and taught to them by their parents, and they too had accepted it, also ready-made from their grandfathers, and the grandfathers from their great-grandfathers, bequeathing in trust the preservation of its wholeness and inviolability, like Vesta's fire.' (97)

---

[1] Cf N.V. Gogol, *Polnoe sobranie sochinenii* (Akademiya nauk SSSR, L., 1937-52), Vol. 1, 111.   See also V.I. Mel'nik, *ibid.*, 36-7.
[2] Cf. Gogol's 'Old-World Landowners', *ibid.*, Vol. 11, 15.

The reader is, therefore, presented with an unsullied life, in all its virginity – a life unaroused, unchallenged by passion. In Gogol's *Old-World Landowners* it is, however, the repressed presence of passion which destroys the idyll, and Oblomov, too, will find that his dream is also threatened by passion, when he meets Olga Ilinskaya.[3]

The inhabitants of Oblomovka laugh like Olympian gods at their own store of anecdotes (103) and the mythological character of their world is reinforced for Oblomov himself by the Russian folklore he learns at his nurse's knee: 'with the simplicity and good nature of a Homer' she recounts the deeds of those 'Russian Achilles and Ulysses' – the heroes of the Russian folk epics, the *byliny* , and relates the story of that 'Russian *Golden Fleece'* – *The Firebird.* Nevertheless, the most powerful story to exercise the imagination of the young Oblomov concerns the good fairy in the form of a pike, who grants an idle young man his every desire, feeds and clothes him and provides him with a beautiful fairy-tale wife, Militrisa Kirbityevna:[4]

> Although later, the adult Ilya Ilich would realise that there were no rivers of milk and honey, no good fairies, and although with a smile he would joke about his nurse's tales, the smile was not genuine, and was accompanied by a secret sigh: for him the fairy tale got mixed up with life, and at times he would unconsciously grieve at the fact that the fairy tale was not life, and life was not a fairy tale. He could not help dreaming of Militrisa Kirbityevna. He felt the constant pull of a place where all they knew about was having a good time, where there were no cares and sorrows. There remained with him for ever the disposition to have a lie on the stove, to walk about a bit in ready-made and unearned clothes and eat well at the expense of a good fairy. (93)

Where the 'Dream of Oblomov' is most at variance with the sterile quasi-idyll of Gogol's *Old-World Landowners* is in the central presence of a child. Everything is seen through the eye of the child, but even more important – the child's eye is absorbing everything it sees:

> His infant mind observed everything that was taking place before him. It penetrated deep into his soul, then grew and matured along with him ...
>
> ... Not a single petty detail or characteristic escaped the enquiring mind of the child. The picture of everyday domestic life engraved itself on his soul. His pliant mind was saturated with living

---

3 See R.A. Peace, *The Enigma of Gogol: An Examination of the Writings of N.V. Gogol and their Place in the Russian Literary Tradition,* Cambridge, 1981, 31-47.
4 The heroine of the Russian fairy tale *Bov-Korolevich.*

examples, and unconsciously sketched out the programme of his life according to the life that surrounded him. (87)

The child watches and observes and sees the pattern of the day; the midday meal that follows the 'well-spent' morning; the deep sleep that follows the midday meal. The importance of such constant observation by the young uninformed mind of the child is given further authorial weight in a passage which in its psychological insight must strike the modern reader as well ahead of its time. Unlike the heroes of Dickens's novels (David Copperfield or Oliver Twist) whose traumatic boyhood experiences appear to have left no psychological traces, Oblomov is entirely shaped by his childhood.[5] Indeed, Goncharov, like a modern psychologist, seems to attribute the values and problems of the adult not merely to the experiences of childhood, but to those of the very first days of life:

> The mind and heart of the child were filled with all the pictures, scenes and manners of this way of life, before he had seen his first book. And who knows, how soon the kernel of a mind begins its development within a child's brain? How can one follow the birth of the first ideas and impressions in a baby's mind?
> Perhaps when a child has still scarcely uttered a word, and perhaps has not yet uttered one at all, is not even walking but is only looking at everything, with that dumb, fixed, childish gaze, which adults call blank, he is already seeing and guessing at the significance and connections of the phenomena of his surrounding sphere, but has just not acknowledged this either to himself or to others. (96)

The 'Dream of Oblomov' is therefore the key to understanding *Oblomovism* and this is why it must be considered as the very kernel from which the novel springs - not merely because of the chronology of the novel's creation, but also in terms of the development of its overall conception. Thus, continuing on from the passage quoted above, we are told: 'His father would never think of checking how many sheaves had been mown or reaped, and call people to account for any back-sliding, but just you hand him his handkerchief a bit slowly, and he would shout about insubordination, and would turn the whole house upside down.' (96)

This attitude to major issues, such as the running of the estate, and to minor matters, such as handkerchiefs, is faithfully reproduced in the opening pages of the novel itself. Oblomov has received a letter from his peasant bailiff telling him of a loss of income through various crop failures. Oblomov summons Zakhar to find the letter for him, but it

---

5 See I. Katarskii, *Dikkens v Rossii: Seredina XIX veka*, M., 1966, 390.

appears to be lost. He then summons him again to find his handkerchief, and when this too cannot be found, appears to take the loss of his handkerchief as much to heart as the loss of the letter. When finally Zakhar points out that he himself is lying on his handkerchief, Oblomov is disconcerted and 'quickly finds another reason to make Zakhar guilty'. (13)

Oblomov is unable to cope with letters in a more general sense: he seems incapable of writing. Thus we are told that 'he had learned about all existing laws and those which had long ago ceased to exist, had taken a course in practical jurisprudence, but when, because of some theft in the house, he had to write a document to send to the police, he took a sheet of paper, a pen, thought and thought, and sent for a scribe.' (53)

Such behaviour seems to be foreshadowed (in the retrospective chronology of the 'Dream') by his father's attitude to writing. When a letter arrives at Oblomovka, it takes his father a long time to open it, and there is even speculation on the dire contents it might contain, but it proves to be a request from a neighbour for a recipe for making beer. When at long last Oblomov senior gets round to writing a reply:

> Profound silence reigned in the house; the servants were ordered not to stamp or make a noise. 'The master is writing,' everybody said in the gently respectful tones in which people speak when there is a death in the house. He had just managed to get down: 'Dear Sir' in a slow slanting manner, with a shaking hand, and as carefully as if he were performing some dangerous act, when his wife appeared. (107)

The letter gets no further once it is discovered how much it will cost to send it. Just so the son: when he attempts to write to his landlord to persuade him not to move him out of his apartment, he fusses about the quality of the paper and the ink, then like his father before him, manages to put down 'Dear Sir ', but actually gets further. Nevertheless he is not pleased with what he has written – the style, he feels, is clumsy – and so the letter, like that of his father, is never sent. Later he even tries to prevail on Tarantyev (of all people!) to write his letters for him (43) and the reason he allows such 'Russian proletarians' as Tarantyev and Alekseyev to sponge on him is again related to the 'Dream': it is precisely because such hangers-on are part of the life of Oblomovka and the 'distant Oblomovkas throughout the country' (35). Tarantyev by his very noisiness and gossiping provides a service – he brings life into Oblomov's quiet lassitude; Alekseyev supplies the opposite need – an unobtrusive, scarcely noticed presence.

In the 'Dream' we also learn about the attitude to reading in Oblomovka. Oblomov's father '...did not consider reading to be any fundamental need, he thought of it as a luxury, the sort of thing it was easy to do without ...' (108) In the opening description of Oblomov's room we learn that there are books lying about open, but that their pages are covered in dust and have turned yellow: 'It was obvious that they had been abandoned long ago.' (10)[6] Oblomov has made only one journey in his life, from Oblomovka to Moscow.[7] There is therefore irony in his claim to Penkin that the books he does read 'are mainly travel books', as there is irony also in the fact that he counters Shtolt's's complaint about the lack of books in his apartment by pointing to a travel book on Africa – with mould on its pages. (134) Later, to Olga, he will claim to be reading *The History of Discoveries and Inventions*, though he has only looked at one page (182) and again this title is a subject for authorial irony: 'With *The History of Discoveries and Inventions* he constantly confused new discoveries in Olga's appearance and character, and discovered occasions for chance encounters with her... '(187)[8]

There is in Oblomov's character a certain timidity and fear, the origins of which can also be traced back to Oblomovka. There superstitions were rife and they believed in all sorts of ghosts and monsters: Ilya Ilyich would himself see later that the world was simple, that corpses did not rise from graves, that as soon as giants appeared they were immediately put into side shows, robbers into gaol; but if belief in ghosts itself disappeared, there remained a sediment of terror and unaccountable sadness (95) and now as a grown man at the beginning of the novel, he seems, in this respect at least, to have receded more towards childhood: 'With the years some sort of childish timidity had returned, the apprehension of danger and evil, which occurred outside the sphere of his everyday existence – the result of having grown unaccustomed to varied external phenomena.' (50)

For all the idyll of the landscape of Oblomovka, there is one place which seems to be the focus for all their supernatural fears – the ravine. It is a place of dread held up before the imagination of the child by his elders, and once, when he is tempted to go there and look over the edge as into the crater of a volcano, all his fears well up inside him, and he flees back to the safety of his nurse (91). Later Goncharov will use the idea of the ravine with similar symbolic sense in his novel with the equally evocative title *The Precipice (Obryv)*. Within the symbolic framework of *Oblomov* itself the concept of the horror and the terror which keeps opening up before the hero is developed, as we shall see, through recurrent metaphors of the abyss (*bezdna* and *propast'* – see Ch. IX).

---

[6] Cf. Manilov in *Dead Souls, Gogol, PSS*, Vol. VI, 25.
[7] This detail is excised from the canonical version of the novel (as presumably at odds with the fact that Oblomov must also have travelled to St Petersburg).
[8] The book in question is presumably: J. Beckmann, *A History of Inventions, Discoveries and Origins*, 2 Vols., London, 1846 (See *L.P.*, 671). Goncharov acquired his own passion for reading travel books from his godfather, who was a retired mariner. See Goncharov, *Sob. soch.*, Vol. 7, 238.

After his bad experiences in the civil service and St Petersburg society Oblomov has locked himself into his own ego ('finally he found that the horizon of his activity and daily existence lay within him himself' (53)). In this, too, he is a typical product of Oblomovka ('Their interests were concentrated on themselves, and did not cross or touch anyone else's' (83)). When the peasants of Oblomovka find a stranger lying in a ditch, they decide it is better not to meddle with him; they go off and leave him to his fate. In similar fashion other people for Oblomov seem to present an ever-present threat, and the word 'others' (*drugie*) is a constant refrain throughout the novel (see Ch. IV). Other people are kept at arm's length and the succession of St Petersburg types who call on Oblomov in Part I are each in turn admonished not to approach too near – they have come out of the cold.

One element of Oblomov's 'residue of fear' is his hypochondria, and again its source can he seen in the molly-coddling he received in Oblomovka, where he grew 'like an exotic plant in a hothouse slowly and languidly' (111), not allowed to go out in the snow. When he does and has a snowball fight with the peasant lads, he is rescued, and wrapped, not only in a sheepskin coat, but in his father's fur coat with two blankets on top.

In later life the most 'trivial complaint' is an excuse for non-action. Thus he claims that he is unable to follow Shtol'ts abroad as he had promised, because a fly has bitten his lip. Such a minor affliction as styes on the eyes assumes the status of a major complaint, and when he becomes thoroughly frightened in his civil service job after sending an important document to Archangel in the Arctic north instead of to Astrakhan in the far south, he manages to get his doctor to support his resignation from the service on medical grounds. Civil service life is anyway not congenial to him. Because of his upbringing in Oblomovka he can only conceive of it as activity imbued with family values – 'In the form of some sort of family occupation, such as, for instance, the lazy noting into a notebook of revenues and expenses, like his father used to do.' (47) The inhabitants of Oblomovka looked on work almost as a punishment for original sin: 'They suffered labour as a punishment placed on our forefathers, but they could not love it, and whenever there was an opportunity they escaped from it, finding that quite possible and necessary.' (97)

In the 'Dream' the inability to take practical steps which involve work is revealed most glaringly in respect of the patriarchal home itself, which seems in reality, and perhaps symbolically, to be undergoing a steady process of disintegration. The gates and the porch need repair. The holes under the porch steps are wide enough to allow pigs through to the cellars beneath, and the whole porch sways underfoot. Nevertheless, when it is pointed out that the porch swayed like this when it was first built, Oblomov's father feels reassured that nothing need be done.

A more serious case is the gallery which runs round the outside of the house. Part of this falls down, but it takes two or three weeks for Oblomov's father even to have the debris moved. His consultations with the joiner lead to nothing, until it is finally pointed out that the rest of the structure is unsafe, and he gives orders for it to be propped up by the 'broken-off pieces' that have fallen to the ground. These 'old broken-off pieces' (*starye oblomki*) seem to evoke the family name itself. Indeed, the scion of the Oblomovs, Ilya Ilich, may be seen as just such an *oblomok*, a remnant of an ancient and disintegrating social fabric, which he is ostensibly trying to prop up, though physically torn away from it through his life in St Petersburg.[9]

As a child Oblomov is not allowed to do anything for himself; he has servants at his beck and call. If he should drop something or want to get something, he is prohibited from doing so. All such activity of a healthy young boy is restrained, and so he grows up expecting to be looked after in every respect. This is the most pernicious influence of his childhood on him: 'His powers, seeking an outlet, turned inwards and, fading, drooped' (111). Oblomov himself feels that his life has been blighted from the beginning: 'From the first moment' that I was aware of myself, I felt that my flame was already dying out' (144) and, as Shtol'ts later tells him towards the end of the novel: 'It began with the inability to put on your socks and it ended with the inability to live.' (306) This is Shtol'ts's main point about the difference between the Russian *barin* and the English gentleman.

A regime in which servants pander to the slightest whim of their young masters not only breeds indolence, it also fosters tyranny. This too begins with the 'putting on of socks'. As a young child he resists his nurse's attempts to perform this service for him, by wriggling and swinging his feet. Later, however, such playfulness takes on more masterful overtones:

> Zakhar, as his nurse used to do, pulled on his socks and put on his shoes, and Ilyusha, now a fourteen-year-old, was only capable of lying down and lifting one leg, then the other, and as soon as something seemed to him to be not as it should be would give a kick to Zakhar's nose. (111)

For all the simplicity and good-nature of Oblomov, there is nevertheless a strong streak of cruelty within him. Its origins are linked to the 'observing eye' of the child in Oblomov's 'Dream', and his childish curiosity about the effects of cruelty. We are told that, when all were asleep at Oblomovka after a hearty meal, the young boy would

---

9 Geiro points to uses of the word *oblomok* (in the sense of 'scion') in Pushkin, Lermontov and Baratynsky. *L.P.*, 536-7. (See also V.I. Mel'nik, 'Filosofskie motivy v romane A. A. Goncharova *Oblomov* (k voprosu o sootnoshenii "sotsial'nogo" i "nravstennogo" v romane', *Russkaya literatura*, 1982, No. 3, 97.

amuse himself by tearing the wings off a dragon fly, and observe what it would do; or he would stick a straw through its body and watch it fly about with this 'embellishment'; he would take pleasure in watching a spider sucking the blood from a fly it had caught, but then would kill both the spider and its prey (90). This motif of the tormenting of insects is a sexual one in Goncharov's writing. Thus in *A Common Story (Obyknovennaya istoriya)* the torturing of a beetle is symbolically linked to the torturing relationship of Nadenka and the hero Aduyev, and in *The Precipice*, the tormenting heroine Vera taunts Vikentyev with 'tearing the wings off "the butterfly" ' – her sister, Marfushka. [10]

The tormenting nature of Oblomov in love is seen quite clearly throughout his relationship with Olga, but especially when at the apparent height of their bliss, he writes her a cruel letter, and feels the need, not only to deal her a blow in this way, but actually to spy on her and observe her reactions as she reads it. We are reminded of the cruel curiosity of Oblomov as a child, an echo reinforced by his observation of insect life as he lies in wait for her in the bushes, and notices the activity of ants, a bumble bee, a cluster of flies sucking sap from a lime tree, and two butterflies 'waltzing' round tree trunks: ' "What a lot of activity!" thought Oblomov, peering at this bustle and listening hard to the tiny sounds of nature, "But on the surface all is so quiet and calm." ' (200)

This same contrast between apparent calm and observable turmoil is taken up in Olga's words of reproach, accusing him of envying her quiet happiness: '... I was so quietly happy, and you hastened to disturb this happiness.' (201) She accuses him of having hidden in the bushes to spy on her to see whether she would cry and how she would cry, whereas, she says, had he been sincere in what he wrote in his letter, he would have gone abroad without seeing her. Oblomov himself is struck by the truth of this statement. (201) He was, in fact, seeking a kind of pleasure from her torment, as we see from his mood on finishing writing the letter: 'He enjoyed the prospect of the day, the novelty of the situation. His heart missed a beat as he listened for a knock at the door. Had the servant come? Was Olga already reading the letter? ...'No, the hall was quiet.' (198) Olga is right when later she accuses him of planning her torments: 'You prepared them and took pleasure in them in advance...you are wicked' (206).[11]

A similar pattern is repeated in many forms throughout their relationship. Thus at the end of Part II he suggests a less honourable alternative to marriage – 'another way' *(drugoi put')* : '...Oblomov was carried away by the demands of his egoism, to seek sacrifices from Olga's heart and to take pleasure in this' *(upit'sya etim)* (224). In Part

---

[10] Cf. Goncharov, *Sob. soch.*, Vol.1, 88-9, Vol. VI, 145.
[11] Nevertheless, A.F. Zakharkin can say of Oblomov: 'There is no despotism or cruelty in him.' Zakharkin, *ibid.*, 100.

III Ch.ll his delaying tactics postponing their wedding cause Olga to be overcome by a sudden faintness, and she has to retire to her room, but once again his curiosity has to be satisfied; he puts his ear to her door and tries to peer through the keyhole. (286)[12]

Oblomov's need to torment those close to him has already been apparent from the opening pages of the novel. He seems to delight in watching Zakhar squirm, and his principal instrument of torture, as it will be with Olga, is words. Once he has discovered that Zakhar cannot stand being called 'venomous' (*yadovityi*) he repeats the word for the pleasure of watching its effect. At the same time it is also made clear that his need to make Zakhar his victim springs from a sense of his own inadequacy: his tirade against 'other people' is an obvious case in point. At the end of Part I Chapter 8, before the onset of the 'Dream', Oblomov regrets this scene with Zakhar and recognises his own inadequacies, when compared to 'other people'. He is tormented by 'useless regrets' (*sozhaleniya*) but nevertheless still feels the need to turn their 'sting' (*zhalo*) against somebody else. That somebody can only be Zakhar once again (78). This process is revealing, not only psychologically, but also linguistically: 'regrets' (*sozhaleniya*) turn into *zhalo* – a 'sting' for others. This ambiguity appears to be reflected in the phrase which is constantly on Zakhar's own lips, when he is faced with his master's reproaches – they are *zhalkie slova*: a phrase usually rendered by translators as 'pathetic words'. *Zhalkie* seems to echo the word for sting *zhalo*, and in fact Zakhar is using the adjective in an older sense of 'complaining' (*cf. zhalobnyi*), but in its modern usage it does indeed mean 'pathetic', 'pitiful'. The comic ambiguity of Zakhar's set response to his master's 'stings' seems to reflect the essential ambivalence of Oblomov's psychological state: that which is 'deserving of pity' is exteriorised into the 'stinging complaint'. There is a moment of ironic recognition at the beginning of Part II Chapter 7, when Oblomov uses the word 'Oblomovism' to castigate Zakhar himself: ' "So that's it!" thought [Zakhar]. "You have thought up another pathetic word (*zhalkoe slovo*) and one we know all about!" ' (167) A similar ambiguity inheres in that other adjective constantly used to describe Oblomov's scenes with Zakhar – they are *pateticheskii* - 'pathetic' in one sense, though a better rendering of the word would be 'passionate', 'emotional'.

The 'Dream', therefore, is offered as an explanation of the adult behaviour of Oblomov, and as well as the particular instances cited above it is clear that the whole atmosphere of Oblomovka, with its heavy emphasis on the values of food and midday sleep, has conditioned the hero's own expectations from life. As Leon Stilman has aptly said:

---

[12] The comedy of this incident is reminiscent of an episode in Gogol's play *Marriage* (Act 1, sc. xvii) when Kochkarev and the other suitors try to look through the keyhole at Agafya Tikhonovna.

'Modern psychopathology also would have invited Oblomov to revisit his childhood to try to identify his "secret enemy".'[13] Nevertheless, there is enough of the idyll in Goncharov's portrayal of Oblomovka for some critics to see it in positive terms.[14] Such a view, however, can take little account of Goncharov's own sly irony, his almost Gogolian suggestion that the life lived at Oblomovka is little more than mere animal existence. The general somnolence which afflicts everyone in the · heat of the afternoon forces the inhabitants of Oblomovka to bed down, like so many animals, in the garden, the hay loft, the stable, and the dogs themselves to creep deep within their kennels. The little vignette of the dog Arapka, sitting all morning gazing out of the window, is immediately followed by a parallel picture: 'Old Oblomov himself is not without activity. He sits the whole morning by the window and strictly observes everything that is done in the courtyard.' (88) The irony is underlined some few pages later in more general terms:

> After tea everybody would occupy themselves with something: some would go to the stream and slowly wander along the bank, kicking pebbles into the water; another would sit up to the window and would follow every fleeting event with his eyes. If a cat ran across the courtyard or a jackdaw flew past, the observer would pursue both of them with his gaze and the tip of his nose, turning his head now to the right, now to the left. So dogs sometimes love to sit for whole days on the window, with their heads in the sun, carefully eyeing everyone who passes. (91)

It is against the values of the world of Oblomov's dream – a world which itself has fallen asleep – that Shtol'ts and Olga wrestle to save Oblomov. The advent of Shtol'ts in the novel coincides with Oblomov's waking from his dream of Oblomovka but, as Shtol'ts soon reminds him, Oblomov's sleep has wider implications, and the awakening must also be spiritual: 'You must come out of this sleep' (*nado zhe vyiti iz etogo sna*) (134), he tells his friend. It is this spiritual awakening which Olga and Shtol'ts strive to achieve in the further course of the novel.

---

[13] See Leon Stilman, 'Oblomovka Revisited', *American Slavic and East European Review*, Vol. VII, 1948, 67.
[14] See, for instance, Apollon Girgor'yev, *Sochineniya*, St Petersburg, 1876, Vol. 1, 423; Druzhinin, *ibid.* and Henry Gifford, *The Novel in Russia: From Pushkin to Pasternak*, London, 1964, 57-64, and Setchkarev, *ibid.*, 153.

Chapter IV

The Problem of the 'Other'

The first relationship with which the novel presents us is that between master and servant. Like Oblomov, though on a different social plane, Zakhar is a figure caught between two epochs with different values – a traditional conservatism and a new disorientating liberalism: 'He belonged to two epochs, and both had placed their stamp upon him. From one he had inherited a limitless devotion to the house of Oblomov, and from the other, and most recent one, a refinement and corruption of morals.' (56)   Just as Oblomov is characterised by his *khalat,* so the grey frock-coat (*syurtuk*) with a rent under the armpit, the grey waistcoat and brass buttons, characterise Zakhar. This hint at a uniform (*poluformennaya odezhda*) (11) which is a faint reminder of the livery he used to wear at Oblomovka is as much the outward manifestation of Zakhar's psychology as is the *khalat* of Oblomov. It, too, looks back to Oblomovka, and yet it only *hints* at the formal livery of a respectful servant. The other features which distinguish Zakhar are the lack of hair on his head, compensated for by the enormous side whiskers, each of which would have been sufficient for three beards. Such grotesque details, in the mannner of Gogol, cast Zakhar as a comic character, and the comedy is carried on from the visual level into the verbal sparring between master and servant, and back to the visual in the slapstick possibilities presented by Zakhar's incredible clumsiness.

The opening pages are not unlike Gogol's play *Marriage* (*Zhenit'ba*), where the idle master Podkolesin keeps summoning his servant Stepan in from the next room to ask him a series of questions obliquely related to marriage.[1] Marriage, of course, is not on the mind of Oblomov – as yet – he is too concerned with two other problems which have suddenly confronted him: his peasant bailiff has sent him less money from the estate, and is obviously cheating him; and his landlord wants him to vacate his apartment. Yet the theme of marriage is obliquely present throughout Part I.

Thus when Oblomov complains about the filthy state of his apartment, Zakhar retorts: 'Everything has been swept and tidied as though for a wedding' (13). Zakhar also reminds his master that he is being driven out of his apartment because of marriage (the landlord plans to knock two of his apartments together for his newly married son), at which Oblomov expresses sad surprise that there are such donkeys who wish to get married (16). The theme is further carried on by Oblomov's first visitor, Volkov, with his tittle-tattle about his own love life and that of his acquaintances. Sudbinsky, the next visitor, is

---

[1] N.V. Gogol, *Polnoe sobranie sochinenii*, Vol. V, 9-12.

more seriously concerned with marriage; he needs money for his own wedding, to which he invites Oblomov to act as best man. He also tells Oblomov of the marriage of a former colleague, Kuznetsov. (22) The last of the succession of visitors in Part I, Tarantyev, not only wants to borrow Oblomov's dress-coat (*frak*) for a wedding ('Rokotov is getting married') (45), but he also suggests a putative marriage as a solution to Oblomov's problems with his bailiff, advising him to write to the Governor to enlist his sympathy for the plight of a supposed wife and twenty children (42). Love and marriage, therefore, form an ever present sub-theme for the action (or lack of it) in Part I. Marriage is driving him out of his apartment, marriage is carrying away his friends and acquaintances and he himself is advised to claim the existence of a wife and and an improbably large family as a device to cope with his other problem – the running down of his estate.

Yet if the relationship between Zakhar and Oblomov looks back to the opening of Gogol's *Marriage*, it also carries on and develops the relationship between Aduyev and his servant Yevsei in *A Common Story*. Yevsei is characterised by his passion for cleaning boots. When he is abused by his master, he too answers back, but only to himself. Like Oblomov, Aduyev uses his servant as an outlet for venting his annoyance and frustration over other matters.[2]

Oblomov, annoyed with himself because it is already half past nine and he has not yet got down to business, summons Zakhar, but then forgets why he has summoned him. Called a second time, Zakhar is about to go off again, but such wilfulness only annoys Oblomov, and he decides that he must have the letter from the bailiff. Zakhar is unable to locate it, so Oblomov, to assert his authority, then tells him, as we have seen, to find his handkerchief. Again Zakhar engages in a half-hearted search which is apparently vain, until in triumph he points to the fact that Oblomov himself is lying on it. This obviously disconcerts his master, but he soon finds 'another reason to make Zakhar guilty '(13) – he complains about the filthy state of the apartment. Other people don't have bugs and moths, he says, why is it that other people's apartments are clean? By way of evidence he points to the German piano tuner who lives opposite. Zakhar's scathing reply may be absurdly comic (the German piano tuner is too poor to have dirt) but the exchange marks the inception of an important motif running through the novel – 'other people'.

It is significant that it is Oblomov who brings up the question of 'others' as an attack on Zakhar and that Zakhar's defence is to point to the social inferiority of 'others'; for this is the very inversion of the

---

2 A similar attitude of master and servant is also recorded by Goncharov in *Fregat Pallada:* his relationship with the sailor Fadeyev. See Goncharov, *Sob. soch.*, Vols. 2 and 3 (especially Vol. 3, 39). There are numerous portraits of servants in *Slugi starogo veka, ibid.*, Vol.7, 316-83. Cf. for instance his teasing of Valentin, *ibid.*, 328-9.

central argument between them which occurs in Chapter 8 of Part I. Between these two contrary arguments Oblomov is in fact confronted by a whole series of 'others': Volkov, the society man; Sudbinsky, the career civil servant; Penkin, the hack writer; and the two 'Russian proletarians' – Alekseyev and Tarantyev. Before all these people Oblomov can feel and express his own moral and social superiority.

The occasion for these visits is the first of May; the weather is marvellous (Penkin has actually written an article on the wonderful weather). (24) Each of his visitors, with the exception of Tarantyev, has come to take Oblomov out to greet the Spring. The first of May is a ceremonial day whose origins go back to pagan beliefs, but this festive occasion, celebrating the awakenening of nature, produces no corresponding arousal in Oblomov. In his eyes these visitors still seem associated with winter: they have all come from the cold, as he tells each one of them. Shortly afterwards he will fall into a deep sleep, in which he returns in dream to his childhood, and there we learn of a ritualistic attitude to Spring, which may well condition Oblomov's present attitude to it: 'They would withdraw from the Spring, would not wish to know it, if they had not at its beginning baked a lark. How could they not know this and not carry this out?' (98)[3] Preparation for the onset of Spring by the baking of 'larks' will also be a feature of Oblomov's later life with Agafya Matveyevna.

At the beginning of the novel, however, the representatives of a more sophisticated metropolitan society perform no such precautionary rituals before they greet the Spring (indeed, as Oblomov later complains to Shtol'ts, it is the importing of oysters and lobsters which defines Spring for the inhabitants of St Petersburg (145)). One after the other they fail to break the spell of Oblomov's hibernation. Indeed their cumulative effect appears to induce at the end a deep and genuine sleep.

Volkov, the society man constantly paying visits to everyone, merely reinforces Oblomov's conviction that to stay at home is to preserve one's human dignity. From Sudbinsky Oblomov is interested to learn about former colleagues, and he shows some emotion when he learns that one of their number, Svinkin, has lost a whole set of documents. We understand why, some thirty-six pages later, when we are told of Oblomov's personal difficulties in the civil service because of his own lack of care with documents. Although Sudbinsky manages to arouse some interest, Oblomov feels that he is misdirecting his energies as a civil servant; he would be better off engaging his talents as a writer. However, under the influence of his next visitor, Penkin, he appears to revise his opinion on the more positive merits of writing.

---

[3] The baking of 'larks' from dough on March 9th was the first ritual of the pagan year, which traditionally began in March. See B.A. Rybakov, *Yazychestvo drevnei Rusi*, M., 1987, 667.

As a topical portrait Penkin is the most revealing of all Oblomov's visitors: it is as though in the clash between them we see the new, more socially aware values of the 1860s in confrontation with the idealistic but solipsistic romanticism of the 1840s, residually embodied in Oblomov himself. It is obvious that Penkin represents the typical hack journalist of the post-Crimean-war period. His themes are indicative: trade; the emancipation of women; but, most of all, he 'fights for the realistic tendency in literature'. He regularly publishes articles and reviews and has just written a story very much in the spirit of the 'denunciatory literature' *(oblichitel'naya literatura)* of the period, about the mayor of a certain town, who resorts to physical violence against his fellow citizens (24). This is apparently what he means by the 'realistic tendency' *(real'noe napravlenie)* in literature. His aesthetic principles seem very close to those of the leading critic of the times, A.N. Dobrolyubov, and are views with which Oblomov appears to disagree (in spite of his creator's later delight with Dobrolyubov's review of the novel).

Penkin throws down the artistic gauntlet: 'What! Will you tell us to depict nature: roses, nightingales or a frosty morning, when everything around is seething and on the move? All we need is the bare physiology of society; we've no time for songs now!' (25) The irony of these anti-art-for-art's-sake sentiments condemning roses and nightingales lies in their closeness to what Dobrolyubov himself would proclaim as his own aesthetic manifesto in the review he wrote of this very novel:

> Here we disagree with the advocates of so-called *art for art's sake*, who believe that the excellent delineation of a leaf of a tree is as important, say, as the excellent delineation of a human character... we shall never agree that the poet who wastes his talent on exemplary descriptions of leaf buds and brooks can be as important as an artist who is able with equal talent to reproduce, say, the phenomena of public life. [4]

The phrase 'the bare physiology of society' is also highly indicative: it links Penkin with that movement in literature, first launched in the 1840s under the banner of the 'Natural School' (with its 'Physiology of St Petersburg' etc.), and which in the 1860s was destined to take on more strident overtones in such socio-literary phenomena as 'denunciatory literature'.[5] When Penkin extols the virtues of a recent work, *A Bribe-Taker's Love for a Fallen Woman (Lyubov' vzyatochnika k padshei zhenshchine)* which he claims has uncovered 'all

---

[4] N.A. Dobrolyubov, 'What is Oblomovschchina?' *Selected Philosophical Essays* (trans. J. Fineberg), Foreign Languages Publishing House, M., 1956, 181)
[5] *Fiziologiya Sankt-Peterburga* ('The Physiology of St Petersburg') was the name of an almanach, associated with the 'Natural School', published in 1845 by the radical editor and poet Nekrasov.

the mechanism of our social movement', and so poetically that at times it is sheer Dante, at others Shakespeare, Oblomov is induced to raise himself on his bed and object: 'Going a bit far, aren't you?' (25) Penkin realises that he has in fact overstated his case, but his own exuberance is as nothing to that of Oblomov, who feels called on to dispute Penkin's coldly rationalistic arguments, and oppose to them arguments of the heart – his own humanitarian values. He gets so carried away in this that he actually gets up from his bed and with blazing eyes almost shouts at Penkin. Now it is Penkin's turn to remind Oblomov that he is 'going a bit far'. Oblomov falls silent, yawns, and slowly lies down again. (26) The episode is comic, yet this spirited defence of human values is the first real sign we have of the qualities of Oblomov's 'heart' which will later be the central feature of Shtol'ts's eulogy of his friend in Part IV.

In rejecting the new school of 'denunciatory literature', Oblomov seems to be guided by the more Gogolian values in social criticism of 'laughter through tears': 'In a story of theirs it is not the "unseen tears" that can be heard, but only crude, visible laughter and malice.' (25) Such writing has nothing to do with art: 'Denounce debauchery and filth, only please do it without any claim to poetry.' (25) He calls on writers to see fellow human beings in those less fortunate than themselves and to love them. Penkin, however, objects:

To love a moneylender, a hypocrite, a thieving or dull-witted civil servant. Do you hear me? What are you saying? It is obvious that you do not occupy yourself with literature,' Penkin said with great heat.' 'No, they must be punished, cast out of civil life, out of society...' (25)

The punishment and elimination of such negative members of society as the moneylender are ideas very much in the air in the 1860s, and Dostoyevsky will give them concrete polemical expression, when his student, Raskolnikov, eliminates (and not only from society) the old moneylender Alyona. There is much, therefore, in this exchange between Oblomov and Penkin which, in its criticism of the literary movement of Goncharov's own day, looks both backwards and forwards.

After this somewhat schematic incursion of a whole series of 'others' into Oblomov's life, Zakhar locks the door on Tarantyev, while his master occupies himself with his daydream of a plan for Oblomovka. There he will also be visited by others, but they will be his 'colony of friends' – fresh-faced, of ruddy complexion, without any cares, and with enormous appetites. It will be eternal summer, eternal gaiety. (62) He is disturbed in his reverie by the street cries of St Petersburg: ' "Akh!" Ilya Ilich sadly sighed aloud, "What a life! How hideous this noise of the capital is! When will that life of paradise that I long for come?" ' One is reminded of Chekhov's three sisters with their dream of an idealised Moscow (the Moscow, significantly, of their childhood), a goal constantly in their minds, which, like Oblomov, they make no effort to attain in reality. It is now, if at any time, that Oblomov has every incentive to return; he is being uprooted from his St Petersburg life, and the pressing problems of his estate demand the immediate implementation of his 'plan', but just as Chekhov's three sisters do not think of boarding a train to realise their dreams, so Oblomov does not think of returning to Oblomovka – except in a dream.

At this point, however, he is visited by his doctor, who, for health reasons, prohibits the only 'labour' in which he now indulges – he is told he must forgo all mental activity: 'But the plan for organising the estate?' Oblomov counters in shock. 'For goodness' sake, am I a block of wood?' (68) The doctor makes a medical prediction: 'If you live two or three more years in this climate, lie about all the time and eat fat and heavy things, you will die of a stroke.' (67)

Oblomov is appalled at the doctor's suggestion that he should go abroad. On the other hand he has no inclination to go back to Oblomovka, yet how is he to face moving to a new apartment in St Petersburg? He asks Zakhar why he suggests such a move, and receives the reply: 'I thought that others, like, are no worse than us, and they move, so we could too.' The reaction in Oblomov is electric – Zakhar's words spark off a whole tirade on 'other people', the echoes of which rumble on throughout the rest of the novel. This reaction is all the more unexpected as the argument about 'others', as we have seen, had already been used in an inverse sense in Chapter I as a weapon against Zakhar. Now, however, he is incensed that Zakhar should compare him to others and feels he must punish him for such insolence. Is he like others? Others are poor, uneducated, barely eat, clean their own boots, have no servants, have to work for their living – has he ever had to work? Has he ever gone short of food? Has he ever in his life put on his own socks? In his angry questioning of Zakhar, he asks him if he really can think that he is like others (*kak ty dumaesh', ya 'drugoi'* ?), only to receive the comically ambivalent reply: 'You are quite other' (*Vy sovsem drugoi!*) (74)

After exhausting his spleen on Zakhar, he falls into musing about 'others':

> He thought more and more deeply about the comparison between himself and 'others'. He began to think and think, and now an idea formed in his mind which was completely opposite to the one which he had presented to Zakhar on 'others'. (77)

He realises that he has accomplished nothing all day, not written the letters he had intended to write, has not even got washed. Another would have written the letters, would not have bothered about moving apartment, would have drawn up the 'plan', would have gone to the estate, and he makes a revealing comparison: ' "Another" would never even put on a *khalat*, was yet a further point to be added to the characterisation of "another" ' (77). He realises that 'his mind and his willpower had long ago been paralysed, and, it seemed, irretrievably so':

> Fruitless regrets about the past, burning reproaches of conscience, lacerated him like needles, and with all his power he tried to rid himself of the burden of these reproaches, to find someone guilty other than himself, and to turn their sting on him. But who? ... ' It is all Zakhar's fault!' he whispered. (78)

But in recollecting the details of the scene with Zakhar, he grows ashamed. He cannot blame Zakhar, much as he has tried to do so:

> Having searched in vain for the inimical principle which prevented him from living as he should, as 'other' people lived, he sighed, closed his eyes, and in a few minutes drowsiness once more began little by little to fetter his feelings. (78)

Shortly after this he falls soundly asleep and receives an answer to his searchings in the dream he has of his childhood.

As we have seen, the theme of others is also raised in the dream in the incident of the stranger left to suffer in the ditch. The inhabitants of Oblomovka want a quiet, regular life; it is for others to thirst for change: 'Why did they need variety, change, chance happenings, which other people begged for? Let others sup that cup, they, the inhabitants of Oblomovka, had no concern for anything. Let others live as they want.' (105)[6] Thus we see that the problem of 'others', as much else in Oblomov's life, returns us to the 'Dream'.

---

[6] It might also be argued that a character for whom 'hell' is other people, and who settles for 'existence' (the Vyborg Side) rather than 'essence' (the ideal Oblomovka) could be seen as a *proto-existentialist*.

Chapter V

Love and the 'Other'

The problem of 'others' for Oblomov really comes to the fore in his relationship with Olga. Through her he attempts to appropriate the values of 'the other', and, indeed, through her very name she seems to be appropriable. Her surname is Il'inskaya – an adjectival form derived from Oblomov's own Christian name Il'ya. She is therefore, on the face of it, *his*. Yet his relationship with Olga is not easy.

She is characterised by her brows and her bold enquiring glance. At first Oblomov feels uncomfortable under this scrutiny, as he tells her: 'I feel that with this glance you are extracting from me everything that I do not wish others to know, especially you.' (155) The ideal woman whom he dreams of as a wife would have a smile, which would be sympathetic to him as her husband, but 'condescending to all others; a glance which would be favourable only to him and modest, even stern towards others'. (159)

For all the attraction he feels towards Olga, he realises that the demands she makes of him are too great. Their relationship becomes increasingly complicated by the concept of 'the other' and his fear of 'others'. Nevertheless, in Part II Chapter 10 the concept of the 'other' comes to him as a salvation, a way out: his relationship with Olga is a mistake – there is 'another' whom she will love (159). In the letter in which he confides this insight he writes that from the beginning he should have told her: 'You have made a mistake. The man before you is not the one for whom you have been waiting, about whom you have been dreaming. Wait, he will come and then you will open your eyes...' (197) The advent of the 'other' will bring her the very awakening that Olga herself appears to promise for Oblomov.

Yet, in spite of the cruel blow administered to their relationship by this letter, reconciliation is still possible, and their association continues, even though it is constantly dogged by the spectre of 'the other' (thus he raises the question again in the final section of Part II Chapter 12). To add to this, there is also the fear of 'others'. Their marriage now seems a foregone conclusion, yet Oblomov is embarrassed and disturbed when he meets other people in Olga's presence; he feels he is the object of their curiosity. Yet he is equally shocked when somebody at the theatre identifies the person in the Il'inskys' box as 'some Oblomov or other, a friend of Shtol'ts's'. (249) He has been reduced to the status of an 'other'.

Even more disturbing, he realises that his forthcoming marriage to Olga is a subject for gossip among the servants. Matters come to a head in a scene with Zakhar which echoes his earlier tirade on 'others' in Part I Chapter 8. Now he denies that he ever intended to get married:

'All that is nonsense, absurdity, lies and slander, do you hear?'
said Oblomov, banging his fist against the table. 'This cannot
happen!'
'Why can't it happen?' Zakhar interrupted dispassionately. 'It's a
normal thing, marriage! It's not just you, everybody gets
married.'
'Everybody!' said Oblomov. 'You are a past master at equating
me with others, and even with everybody! This cannot happen!
No, nothing has happened!' (252)

Oblomov launches into a long definition of what marriage means,
and when to Oblomov's arguments on the financial implications of
taking such a step, Zakhar incautiously objects: 'Well, how do other
people with three hundred serfs get married?' (252) an incensed
Oblomov rehearses all the old arguments about the difference between
himself and others.

If his intention had been to frighten Zakhar and stop his tittle-tattle
about a wedding, the real result is that he frightens himself, and talks
himself out of the idea of the marriage. Yet, if the fear of 'others' is a
decisive factor in the cooling of his relationship with Olga, it is the
presence of 'another', Agaf'ya Matveyevna Pshenitsyna, which makes
the break inevitable.

In reality, that 'other' posited in Oblomov's letter of self-doubt to
Olga, and referred to more than once after the ensuing reconciliation,
is, of course, Oblomov's 'other pole' – Shtol'ts, and it is significant that
later in the novel Shtol'ts himself will make use of Oblomov's letter to
persuade Olga that Oblomov had actually foreseen and predicted that it
was he she should marry. (326)

It was Shtol'ts who had first introduced Oblomov to Olga. At the
beginning of Part II, when Shtol'ts has returned to wake Oblomov from
his dream, he gets him to recount his other dream – that idyllic new life
on his estate, which he will enjoy once his plan has been worked out.
Shtol'ts cannot see any difference between this supposedly idyllic life
and that lived by Oblomov's father and grandfather, but Oblomov
objects, and appears to suggest that the difference will lie in those
elements of western civilisation that characterise his own education and
his later association with St Petersburg: there will be music, books, a
grand piano and elegant furniture. He paints the picture of an evening
meal followed by music:

'There will be music there. Casta diva... Casta diva!' Oblomov
began to sing, 'I cannot think about Casta Diva without being
moved!' he said, when he had sung the beginning of the Cavatina.
'How the heart of that woman sobs! What grief permeates these
sounds! And nobody around her knows anything at all... she is

alone... her secret weighs her down; she entrusts it to the moon.'
(141-2)

When Shtol'ts learns that his friend likes this aria, he promises to
introduce him to Olga Ilinskaya, who, he says, sings it beautifully,
admitting, at the same time, that he himself has a weakness for her.

So, from the beginning, Olga is identified with the Casta Diva, the
'chaste goddess' of Oblomov's other dream – his 'plan', and we note that
in this identification the goddess is not only 'chaste', but associated with
suffering womanhood ('how the heart of that woman sobs, what grief
permeates these sounds!') We also note Shtol'ts's confession of
partiality for Olga herself, and perhaps even more significantly we
become aware of another possibility for love in Oblomov's picture of
the ideal life – love not on the exalted plane of the Casta Diva, but slyly
focused on a bare-foot peasant girl 'with a sunburned neck, and bare
elbows, with eyes timidly lowered, but saucy, scarcely imperceptibly,
out of mere seemliness, shunning the master's advances, but in herself
quite glad... Sh! You don't want the wife to see. God forbid!' (141) The
moment has been anticipated in Part I Chapter 8, after Oblomov's
reveries had been interrupted by the street cries of St Petersburg:

'When will that longed-for life of paradise come? When can I go
to the fields and my native groves?' he thought. 'I would like to
be lying on the grass now, under a tree, and looking at the sun
through the branches, counting how many birds visit its branches,
and then either dinner or lunch would be brought to me on the
grass by some rosy-cheeked servant girl with bare, soft round
elbows and sunburned neck; the saucy girl would lower her eyes
and smile...When will that time come?...' (63)

If 'The Dream of Oblomov' contains all the seeds of Oblomov's
psychological and spiritual condition, all the embryonic shoots for the
future plot are to be found in the 'waking dream' recounted in Part II
Ch.4. Here is the unattainable goddess, whose true worth is appreciated
by Shtol'ts himself, whereas for Oblomov her chaste attractiveness,
linked to female suffering, yields before the 'bare elbows' and more
bucolic charms of a woman of lower social status (he is first aware of
Agafya Matveyevna as a woman 'with a bare neck and elbows' (232)
and the folklore of Oblomovka interprets a tickling in the elbow as a
prediction that one will sleep in a new place (104)). It is for this 'dream'
– the idyllic daydream – that Shtol'ts first coins the word 'Oblomovism'
(*Oblomovshchina*), a term which takes on an even more negative
interpretation as the novel progresses.

By the end of the same chapter (Part II Chapter IV) Shtol'ts himself
appears to have re-defined the term to cover Oblomov's procrastination
and general inability to take action. He leaves him with a choice: 'Now

or never', and these are the very words which run through Oblomov's head when he wakes up the following morning, and sees Shtol'ts writing in the drawing room. He himself sits down at his desk to write, but there is neither ink nor paper. Instead he finds himself mechanically writing in the dust, and the word he has written is *Oblomovshchina*: 'he dreamed of this word at night, written in letters of fire on the walls, as at Belshazzar's feast'. (146)

It hardly augurs well for his budding relationship with Olga, that at the opening of Chapter 7 he is again writing in the dust – but this time the word is 'Olga'. Then realising how dirty his *dacha* is and that he has been criticised for this by Olga herself, he summons Zakhar in to clean it, with words that add further to the symbolic significance of this little scene: 'This is revolting. This is Oblomovism.' (166)

The *Oblomovism* which has dogged his relationship with Olga throughout is defined as the cause for everything in their final scene of parting:

> 'Why has everything gone wrong?' she suddenly asked, raising her head. 'Who has put a curse on you, Ilya? What have you done? You are kind, intelligent, gentle, noble and ... and here you are perishing! What has ruined you? This evil has no name.'
> 'It has,' he said, scarcely audibly.
> She looked at him questioningly, her eyes full of tears.
> 'Oblomovism!' he whispered ... (290)

Earlier in the novel, however, Shtol'ts's challenge 'now or never' echoes through Oblomov's mind. It becomes for him more profound than the Hamlet question: 'To be or not to be?' (147) He does not follow Shtol'ts abroad, as he had promised, or even reply to his letters. Perhaps, speculates the author, 'In the ominous cry: "now or never", Ilya Ilyich had fixed on the latter.' Yet this is not entirely the case – under the influence of Olga, Oblomov has become a new man. (148)

Ominously, however, 'never' becomes a key word in this amorous relationship. It begins to assume this role in Part II Chapter 8 when Oblomov refuses to tell Olga why he likes the fact that she is annoyed. To blackmail him into telling her, she even starts to sing 'Casta Diva', but he becomes even more adamant: 'Not for anything! Never! What if it is not true? What if it just seemed like this to me? Never, never!' (172)

In Chapter 10 after Oblomov has sent his cruel letter, there may be reconciliation, but it is now Olga's turn to utter the ominous word 'never'. He asks for a kiss but she steps back, her eyes blazing: ' "Never, never! Don't come near me!" she said in fright, almost in terror, stretching out her two arms and her parasol between herself and him.' (206) Yet when she sees 'What sanctity her "never" had for Oblomov'

(206) her anger yields place to pity, but Oblomov, for his part, feels he has ruined everything:

'I have spoilt everything! That was a real mistake! "Never!" Oh, Lord, the lilacs have faded,' he thought, looking at the hanging lilacs. 'Yesterday has faded, the letter has also faded, and this moment, the best in my life, when for the first time a woman said to me, like a voice from heaven, that there is something good in me, –that too has faded!' (207)

He asks for forgiveness, but she is silent:

'That ominous "never!" ' he said sadly, and gave a sigh. 'It will fade,' she whispered, scarcely audibly, blushing. (207)

Thus we see that this ominous 'never' is linked with that other symbol of their love – 'lilac'.[1]

In Chapter 12 Olga again tries to get Oblomov to speak out his mind. She grabs him by his coat lapels, and he has to turn away in order not to kiss her: 'He would have liked not to turn away, but there thundered in his ears her ominous "never".' (218)

By the end of the chapter Oblomov has proposed marriage to her, and when she then tells him that she had thought of him as her husband from the moment that she had given him the lilac branch, he opens his arms to embrace her, but once more she fends him off with her parasol, and we read: 'He remembered the ominous "never", and became docile.' (223)   Having offered marriage, Oblomov is disappointed at her lack of emotion, particularly at her lack of tears, and a serpent of doubt within him prompts him to make another suggestion. There is another way, he says, hinting that instead of marriage, she could become his mistress. Once more he encounters the fateful 'never ':

'You would like to know whether I would sacrifice my peace of mind for you, by going along this road with you? Isn't that true?'
'Yes, it seems you have guessed... What then?'
"Never", not for anything! she said firmly.' (223)

But Oblomov persists: it would be the ultimate way of showing her love – she would despise the opinions of others (a feat he himself is unable to accomplish!):

---

[1] Ehre stresses a more positive link to the theme of 'lilacs': 'Light and lilacs in their frequent repetition become lyrical refrains through which Goncharov strives to suggest what he calls "a poem of love".' Ehre, 185.

'Why do you say such terrible things to me?' she said calmly, 'I will never go along that road.'
'Never?' asked Oblomov, despondently.
'Never!' she repeated. (224)

Oblomov persists in his torture, but Olga is unmoved, and when he asks her why it is that she will not go along that road, if, as she claims, it does not frighten her, there is an unexpected new twist to the 'never' of her reply:

'Because on this road, people ...later, always... part,' she said.
'And I...can part with you!'
She stopped, placed her hand on his shoulder, looked at him a long time, and suddenly throwing aside her parasol, swiftly and passionately twined her arms around his neck, kissed him, then flushed all over, pressed her face to his chest, and added softly, 'Never!' (224)

Thus on this strange symbolic reconciliation of 'never', used in two contrary senses, Part II ends with Oblomov falling down at Olga's feet.

In Part III Oblomov returns home to find Tarantyev waiting for him to persuade him to move to the house of Agafya Matveyevna on the Vyborg side of the river. He cannot get out of it, he has signed a contract, claims Tarantyev. The suggested move is an obvious threat to that other contract which appears to have been concluded at the end of Part II. When Oblomov has got rid of Tarantyev, he muses on the significance of what has passed between himself and Olga: 'Two "nevers",' he said, quietly, with joyful emotion, 'and what a difference between them: one has already faded, and the other has blossomed so luxuriantly.' (228) But already he begins to have doubts. The prospect of marriage appears to make love itself fade and lose its rainbow hues. (228)

At the end of Chapter 4, when he has renounced marriage, frightened by his own tirade to Zakhar on 'others', he realises how differently he had planned breaking his news to Zakhar: ' "It has faded, gone away," echoed inside him. "What is there now?"' (256) These very words are repeated by Olga during their final, emotional scene of parting (Part III Chapter 11): ' "No, let me cry! I am not crying about the future, but about the past," she said with difficulty. "It has faded, gone away." ' (289)

The final 'never' is pronounced on him by Shtol'ts, when in Part IV Chapter 2 he visits him at the house of Agafya Matveyevna for his nameday celebrations.

'Well, Ilya?!' he said at last, but so sternly, so questioningly, that Oblomov averted his gaze and kept silent.

'It's therefore "never"?'
'What do you mean, "never"?' Oblomov asked, as though not understanding.
'You have already forgotten! "Now or never!" ' (303)

In his portrayal of the love between Oblomov and Olga Goncharov makes skilful use of the language of flowers to hint at that which cannot be uttered. Thus at the end of Part II Chapter 3 Olga had quite unexpectedly forced a declaration of love from Oblomov:

> But she knew why his face bore such an expression, and inwardly she felt a modest triumph, admiring this expression of her power. 'Look in the mirror,' she continued, with a smile showing him his face in the mirror. 'Your eyes are shining. Goodness, there are tears in them! How deeply you feel music!...'
> 'No, I feel...not music...but...love!' said Oblomov quietly. (159)

The moment is one of acute embarrassment for them both. Each has really gone too far, but there is surely an intended irony in the fact that Oblomov makes his declaration of love to his own face in the mirror. Confused at his boldness, Oblomov beats a hasty retreat. Both are filled with disturbingly contrary emotions, and their next meeting will obviously be difficult. Olga rehearses the sort of pained but provocative reply that her friend Sonechka would have given, but when they next meet (by accident?) in the park, she is unable to say what she intended and Oblomov is tongue-tied. Olga breaks off a lilac branch and is able to hide her face in it as she smells it. She invites Oblomov to smell it too, but he, confused and wishing to distance himself from his earlier impulsive declaration, rather ungallantly says that lilies of the valley have a better scent – lilac is cloying. He picks, and offers her, lilies of the valley, but again undoes the gallantry of the gesture, by confessing that he does not like flowers at all – in the house they are a source of trouble and dirt. This remark allows Olga to sting him in her turn with a question about the cleanliness of his own living quarters.

Oblomov tells her that he is leaving next day – 'from shame' – and that what he had said the evening before was 'untrue'. At the word 'untrue' Olga drops her flowers. She may not have been able to say what she intended, but the apology has been given, without it. Oblomov's emotions, he suggests, derived from nothing more than the influence of the music. According to her earlier views on the matter she should now feel relieved:

> 'So it's nothing! So he has taken back his incautious word, and there is no need to be angry! Well, that's good ... now it's all right. We can talk as we did before, and joke,' she thought and, in passing, wrenched a branch from a tree, and with her lips tore

a small leaf away. Then immediately she threw both the branch
and the leaf on the path. (164)

Oblomov thinks this display of anger derives from the original
incident, but when she reassures him that she has already forgotten it, he
is at a loss to explain the cause of her annoyance, as apparently is Olga
herself. She rationalises it as a reaction to her inability to say what she
had intended; that Oblomov had pre-empted her, that he had the
temerity to lie to her.

When she leaves, Oblomov wanders round the park on his own, and
in retracing his steps along the avenue where he had walked with Olga,
he comes across the lilies of the valley and the lilac branch she had torn
off so violently:

'Why did she do that?' he began to speculate, and to recall ...
'Fool, fool!' he suddenly said out loud, seizing the lilies of the
valley and the branch, and rushing, almost running along the
avenue. 'I asked her forgiveness and she ... oh, surely not? What
a thought!' (166)

Oblomov returns home in exaltation, and it is then that he writes
Olga's name in the dust of his desk.

After examining himself in the mirror once more, and liking what
he sees (170), he is invited to dinner at Olga's house. Olga comes to
meet him and she notices that Oblomov is carrying a lilac branch. In
response to her cross-questioning, he replies that it is the one she threw
down and that he likes it because she threw it down in annoyance. She
asks him whether he likes 'annoyance', but he refuses to tell her, even
though she tries on him the charm of music – singing the opening of
'Casta Diva'. Oblomov, however, is firm and, as we have seen, counters
with his symbolic word 'never' (172).

There is, however, the suggestion of a further image complicating
his relationship with Olga: the origin of the motif of 'lilacs' is to be
found in Oblomov's dream, where it seems to suggest another Casta
Diva – the ideal of saintly, unattainable womanhood; for the scent of
lilac is associated with the memory of his dead mother and the
recollection of her instructing him to pray (85).

The bench near the place where Olga broke off the lilac branch
becomes an obvious focus for the assignations of Olga and Oblomov
(181). Yet it seems significant that in their developing relationship the
language of flowers ostensibly symbolises negative emotion. The torn
lilac branch is a mark of anger, yet in reality it masks an
acknowledgement of love. There could, perhaps, be no more telling
symbol of Olga's love for Oblomov, which is destined to flounder in
frustration, annoyance and anger.

Olga, for her part, is concerned with reforming Oblomov. She gently reproves him for eating huge suppers, and as she does so, she works at a piece of embroidery – a bell pull, for which the motif is a sprig of lilac. She claims that she selected this particular motif by chance, and the bell pull is for the baron (later Zakhar will report gossip that she is to marry the baron, and after the break with Oblomov, the baron does indeed propose).

During this scene Oblomov is not in a happy frame of mind; he feels he needs a further admission from Olga. As they walk to the grove he complains of a lack of aim in his life:

> 'For what and for whom shall I live?' he said, following behind her. 'What is there to look for, and to what can I direct my thoughts and my intentions? Life's blossom has fallen, only the thorns remain.'
>
> They went along slowly; she listened absent-mindedly. In passing she tore off a lilac branch and gave it to him without looking at him.
>
> 'What is that?' he asked, growing numb.
>
> 'You can see what it is – a branch.'
>
> 'What sort of branch?' he said looking at her with bulging eyes.
>
> 'Lilac.'
>
> 'I know...But what does it mean?'
>
> 'Life's blossom and...'
>
> He stopped, and so did she.
>
> 'And?' he repeated questioningly.
>
> 'My annoyance,' she said, looking directly at him with a concentrated gaze, and her smile said that she knew what she was doing. (183-4)

This is the reinforcement of the acknowledgement of love, which he needs. Once more he is happy, but significantly the lilac branch, as a token of love, is actually an expression of 'annoyance':

> 'Life, life, again it opens up to me,' he said as though in a feverish dream. 'It is there in your eyes, in your smile, in this branch, in Casta Diva...Everything is here.' (184)

Neverthless, in an oblique reference to the need for marriage, Olga reminds him that this is not all, only half.

Now their relationship enters a new phase:

> The moment of symbolic hints, significant smiles, lilac branches had passed never to return. Love became sterner, more

demanding, and began to turn into a sort of obligation. The question of mutual rights arose. (188-9)

Olga prods him about his laziness and his wasted years, but Oblomov has not yet got round to a serious proposal of marriage. He appears to expect Olga to make all the concessions, and in Part II Chapter 10, when he suddenly has his grave misgivings about their relationship, he feels the blame is hers. She is too slow in love and the image of her at work, embroidering the lilac sprig, whilst at the same time upbraiding him for his laziness, seems now to suggest a new analogy: 'She loves now in the way in which she embroiders, the pattern comes out slowly, lazily, she unfolds it even more lazily, admires it, and then she will put it down and forget it.' (195)

In the letter he writes her, he says that the light, smiling apparition of their love with its sounds of Casta Diva and its scent of lilac has gone. He implies that he can no longer face up to the serious implications of their love. Reconciliation follows after the trauma of this letter, and their love as a consequence has matured, like the summer season itself. A recurrent theme now is 'the lilacs have faded and gone' . By Chapter 11 not only the lilacs, but the lime trees have 'ceased blooming' (*ottsveli*) and the berries have gone. Their romance ends in midwinter, when the earth, like Oblomov himself, seems locked into inertia and increasingly more cold.

After their final break the moratorium imposed on Oblomov's life seems to be epitomised by the snow falling at the end of Part III. As though in a daze he repeats the word: 'Snow, snow, snow...It has covered everything' (291). He falls ill and, as he recovers at the beginning of Part IV, keen grief is replaced by dumb indifference, which again seems to find its symbolic equivalent in the blanket of snow covering the outside world (293). The dream of happiness with Olga has ended (much as the dream of his childhood) in a world of winter which forces him to take to his bed. (112)

The motif of the lilac resurfaces, however, in the romance of Olga and Shtol'ts. She tells him of her love for Oblomov and of the significance of the lilac. (325) She feels that this past might stand in the way of her new love for Shtol'ts, but he reassures her, using the very symbols of the old love: 'It will fade, like your lilac. You have had a lesson, now the time has come to put it to use.' (329)

Thus the negative aspects lurking behind this symbol of their love, a love predicated on 'never', are finally brought home to her. It was a plant doomed to fade (as Oblomov seemed to predict). It provides merely a lesson, a preparation for that 'other' man who was to come along.

Yet Oblomov himself is not forgotten even in death; for we read that: 'branches of lilac, planted by a friendly hand, slumber over his grave.' (376).

Chapter VI

Olga

The fact that Olga should marry Shtol'ts is not entirely unexpected, it is in a sense 'prepared' at the very beginning of her relationship with Oblomov. Thus almost from the first she tells Oblomov:

'I like Andrei Ivanovich ... not only because he makes me laugh, sometimes when he speaks, I cry; and not because he likes me, but perhaps because he likes me more than anyone else. You see how far my egoism has gone!'
'You like Andrei?' Oblomov asked her, and his glance, intense and quizzical, looked straight into her eyes. 'Yes, of course, if he likes me more than anyone else, then there's no question of my not liking him,' she replied gravely. (157)

This interchange in the Russian original seems even clearer, as the verb 'to like' (*lyubit'*) is actually the verb 'to love'. The nature of such 'love' seems to be further defined, for she goes on to say that Andrei talks to her like a sister, but then corrects herself: 'No, like a daughter.' (157)

For all her apparent independence and self-assurance, Olga still feels the need of advice from a more experienced person. She regards Shtol'ts as a mentor. Her own aunt, it is made clear, is not the sort of person to provide guidance, and in Shtol'ts's absence Olga therefore turns to her married friend Sonechka. She cannot seek the help of Oblomov himself; for, in a telling comparison, he is described as a sort of Galatea for whom she has to be a Pygmalion (186).[1]

Nevertheless before the completion of her 'sentimental education' at the hands of Oblomov, the gulf between her and Shtol'ts seems very great:

She remembered the prediction of Shtol'ts: he frequently said to her that she had not yet begun to live, and sometimes she took offence at the fact that he considered her a young girl, whereas she was in fact twenty. But now she understood that he had been right, that she had only just begun to live. (186)

---

[1] In Greek mythology Pygmalion was a sculptor, who fell in love with a statue which he had made. The goddess Aphrodite brought the statue to life, and under the name of Galatea the statue became Pygmalion's wife.

In her relationship with Oblomov she is forced all the time to take the dominant role, and there is constant reference to imagery of resurrection and awakening. At the same time her love is both a 'task' and a 'lesson':

> He would live, act, bless his life and her. To return a person to life - what glory for a doctor, when he saves someone who is hopelessly ill! But to save a mind which is perishing morally, to save a soul? ...
> She would even shudder, trembling with pride and joy. She considered it a task assigned from above. In her thoughts she made him her secretary, her librarian. (161)

The word *urok* ('task') is ambiguous – it also means 'lesson' – and this is to be the final evaluation of the relationship: it has really been a 'lesson'. Yet if this is 'a lesson assigned from above', it is she who instructs. She bullies him and coaxes him out of eating supper (a provincial custom frowned on in St Petersburg, as we learn from *A Common Story*) [2] ; she prevents him from lying down, makes him take walks, climb hills. His personal attire improves, as does the general cleanliness of his living quarters. She improves his education, as well as her own, by making him read books, which they can then both discuss.

In the characterisation of Olga the 'female question' (*zhenskii vopros*) of the post-Crimean-War period is never far away. There are undoubted gaps in her education on matters which it is not considered necessary for women to know (190), and in such matters it is Oblomov's turn to become her 'professor'. She sends him into St Petersburg to consult books and the art gallery of the Hermitage, so that afterwards he can relate his findings to her. She also sends him to shops to buy engravings of pictures of note.

The love of Olga for Oblomov, which Shtol'ts later finds so surprising (even though Oblomov himself holds Shtol'ts responsible for inoculating them with the virus (264)), is perhaps not so strange after all. The relationship is complementary. Olga persists with Oblomov against all the odds precisely because she can dominate him, and Oblomov, for all his misgivings, enjoys being dominated. As we have seen, Oblomov's first declaration of love is blurted out, when she herself is secretly admiring her power over him. (159)

Perhaps the most telling image (although it is hardly flattering to Oblomov himself) occurs in Part II Chapter 8: 'She had weighed up her power over him in a moment, and she liked her role of a guiding star, a ray of light, which she would shed on a stagnant lake and be reflected in it.' (182)

---

[2] In *Fregat Pallada* Goncharov himself tells us that he does not have supper. Goncharov, *Sob. soch.*, Vol. 3, 381.

We have seen that there is something of the tormenting child in Oblomov's attitude towards Olga's emotions, but there is also something provocative, teasing, even tormenting in her attitude towards him. It is there from the start in her gently sarcastic teasing of him for his way of life and social gaucheness. It is there in her bold penetrating look, and particularly in her quizzical eyebrows – one higher than the other – a feature presented as a constant physical motif in her characterisation. When at the end of Part II Chapter 5 her teasing has caused Oblomov to blurt out his love, there is a significant element of regret about the new seriousness this has introduced into their relationship:

> It seemed she was sorry that something had happened which prevented her from tormenting Oblomov, by training on him an inquisitive glance, and good-naturedly wounding him with joking remarks about lying down, about laziness, and about his clumsiness... (160)

Nevertheless during the next stage of their relationship we are told that: 'Olga, like all women in the dominant role, that is the role of a "tormentor", of course less than others and unconsciously, could not deny herself the pleasure of playing with him a little, as a cat does.' (182)[3] We are also told that the closer she grew to him 'she changed from sarcasm directed at Oblomov's languid and flabby existence, to a despotic demonstration of will.' (189) Whenever he prepared to yawn, she would fix him with such an astounded stare, that he would immediately close his mouth and so violently that his teeth would clash together. (189)

Often, however, her teasing is more playful. At the beginning of Part II Chapter 12, we see her running on ahead, refusing to let Oblomov catch up with her, and laughing at him as he struggles behind her (217). Later in St Petersburg she forces him to take her out in a boat on the coldly autumnal river Neva, despite his protestations that he is not dressed warmly enough for such an outing, and once they are on the river she playfully splashes him with cold water. (259) All this shows the mettlesome spirit of a young girl – but it evokes a fear of boats expressed earlier. (50) [4] Moreover, the symbolism of this chilly scene inverts the poetry of that blissful episode in the dream of married life which Oblomov had earlier described to Shtol'ts: it would be a hot summer's evening; he and his wife would be on the river, and she (significantly) would be steering. (140)

---

[3] For a discussion of animal imagery in the novel see Setchkarev., *ibid.,* 158.
[4] 'In a throng he felt suffocated, and would get into a boat with the uncertain hope that he would get safely to the other shore....' (50)

The problem with Oblomov is that he can never properly break out of this 'daydream'; Olga, on the other hand, is 'learning love'. For her it is a process, whereas for Oblomov it is a state:

> Oblomov did not learn love. He would fall asleep in that sweet slumber of his, about which, in the presence of Shtol'ts, he had once daydreamed aloud. At times he would begin to believe in a constantly cloudless life, and again he dreamed of Oblomovka peopled by kind friendly people without a care in the world, [he dreamed] of sitting on the terrace, of deep musings which came from the fullness of satisfied happiness. (214)

Giving himself up to this dream he has on a couple of occasions fallen asleep in the wood whilst waiting for Olga. (214) Although Oblomov has this static view of his own role in their relationship, which is conditioned by his daydream of happiness, he is nevertheless constantly seeking reassurances, further sacrifices and concessions from Olga.

The analysis of their emotions which takes place in Part II Chapter 9 hinges on the difference between 'loving' and 'being in love'. Olga insists that she loves Oblomov, but does not like the idea of being in love: "'I lo..ove!" Oblomov pronounced. "But, after all, one can love one's mother, father, nurse, even a pet dog: all this is covered by the general collective concept 'I love', as by an old...'"(191) Olga supplies the missing word, in her teasing manner, by suggesting that the 'old' multipurpose covering which Oblomov has in mind is 'dressing-gown' (khalat). She tries to get out of Oblomov's emotional cross-questioning by changing the subject, but Oblomov rebukes her: the difference between 'loving' and 'being in love' is of great importance to him – significantly one is an active verb (ya lyublyu), the other is passive, an achieved state (ya vlyublen – a passive past participle). Yet Olga's explanation of the difference appears to invert this linguistic and logical distinction: 'You see, you need every day to renew the store of your tender feelings! That's where the difference lies between one in love and one who loves' (vot gde raznitsa mezhdu vlyublennym i lyubyashchim). (191) Olga is right: Oblomov's 'state of love', that idyll branded by Shtol'ts as 'Oblomovism', is not yet an achieved state – he needs constant reassurances that what he is experiencing is actually going to turn into the 'reality' of his dream. His passive state of 'being in love' can only be based on the active love of his partner.

Nevertheless, Oblomov persists in seeing the difference as one of intensity and degree of feeling, and since Olga says that she loves, but is not prepared to say that she is in love, he calls her words 'almost like those of Cordelia' (eto slova...kak budto Kordelii!) (191). He thus identifies her with the daughter of King Lear, who honestly and plainly answered her father's question about loving him, and as a result suffered for it. When Oblomov goes on to question her about her view of life, she replies:

> 'Life is duty, obligation, therefore love is also a duty. It is as though it has been sent to me by God,' she added, raising her eyes heavenwards, 'and He has ordered me to love.'
> 'Cordelia!' Oblomov pronounced aloud. 'And she but twenty-one! So that's what love is in your opinion!' he added in deep thought. (192)

The image of Cordelia is, of course, ultimately reassuring; for her love proved to be genuine, even though honestly and bluntly professed. The idea of Olga's love as duty and 'God-sent' also has its appeal for Oblomov, but the idea of life as duty and obligation smacks too much of Shtol'ts's puritan ethic for him to be entirely happy with it:

> In reality Oblomov was not at all concerned whether or not Olga were Cordelia, or whether she would remain true to this image, or would set off on another path and turn into a different vision, provided she appeared in the light and colours in which she lived in his heart, provided he was happy. (193)

The main thing is that Olga should conform to the daydream – the static ideal of a loving wife.

Olga, for her part, does not seek chivalric tokens of active love from Oblomov, 'If only he remained true to the ideal of a man, a man, moreover, awakening to life through her.' (193-4)   Olga's ideal of love, then, is not a static state, but one of movement and improvement. In this mutual analysis of their emotions there is much that could disturb Oblomov. Nevertheless, for all that Oblomov might wish it, he cannot in fact reduce his own emotions to an idealised stasis. The chapter ends on a premonitory note:

> And therefore in the fleeting image of Cordelia, in the fire of Oblomov's passion there had been reflected just one moment, one ephemeral breath of love, merely its morning, a single capricious pattern. But tomorrow, tomorrow another moment would shine, just as beautiful, perhaps, but all the same another one. (194)

The morrow is indeed a different day; it brings Oblomov's self-doubts and his cruel letter. Nor can Olga maintain the Cordelia image and the soberly rational analysis of emotion for long. In Chapter 11 walking arm in arm with Oblomov in the heat of midday, she finds herself succumbing to a passionately languid state, which, on the face of it, is not too dissimilar from Oblomovism itself. She lazily leans on Oblomov's shoulder, walks along mechanically in a state of enervation:

'All energy ebbed from her, her wearied, lifeless glance became static, focused on some object or other, and she hadn't the energy to direct it anywhere else.' (210) Her clothing seems to oppress and squeeze her, and she feels she could just lie down under a tree and stay there for hours.

This state reaches a climax one hot sticky evening. In a 'lunacy of love' *(lunatizm lyubvi)* she takes Oblomov out into the garden; talks of vague fears and of her fear of him; squeezes up to him; gets him to put his hand on her beating heart; seizes him by the shoulders; asks him to cover her eyes; and lays her head on his shoulder, so that he feels her hot breath on his cheek. Oblomov, in alarm, wants to go back to the house, but she says that her heart is burning, and she squeezes his hands, looking closely into his eyes from time to time. Then she begins to sob. With these tears, she says, the fire will leave her. Oblomov hears her heavy breathing in the darkness, feels her hot tears on his hand, and her convulsive grip. Her head is on his shoulder and her breath burns his cheek. He, too, trembles, but he dare not touch her cheek with his lips. Finally they return to the house, and as he takes his leave, he notices her sultry *(zharkii)* smile: 'He had seen that smile somewhere; he recalled some picture or other, which depicted a woman with just such a smile...Only it wasn't Cordelia. '(212)

Later when Olga tells Shtol'ts about her love for Oblomov, significantly, this is the one incident which she leaves out: 'But she passed over the sultry evening in the garden in silence...probably because she had not yet been able to decide what sort of an attack she had had then.' (325)

The morning after this 'lunacy of love' Olga seems to have recovered, but her mood can change, and just as Oblomov himself had had doubts about their love, so when Olga begins to ponder their relationship, she too is assailed by doubts; the 'fairy-tale world of love' is capable of turning into an autumn day, when everything takes on a grey coloration. There is here an echo of the grey day experienced by Oblomov at the opening of Chapter 10, and the reference to autumn seems ominous. Whatever doubts Olga may have, she feels that she has already committed herself too far, and in an image reminiscent of the central symbol of Oblomovism itself, the *khalat*, she concludes: 'One cannot discard love on a whim, like a dress', (214) but she gives no hint to Oblomov of her struggle and her doubts. One of the arguments in her struggle with herself is the concept of love as duty and commitment: ' "One doesn't love twice in a life," she thought. "That, they say, is immoral."' (214) It is this idea of immorality which she needs to overcome, before she can bring herself to think of marrying Shtol'ts, even though her relationship with Oblomov has long faded. In the final scene of their parting Olga admits, rather ominously, that what she had loved in Oblomov was what Shtol'ts had shown her, and what she and

Shtol'ts had thought up together: 'I loved the future Oblomov,' she confesses. (289)

Oblomov is the eternal child; he refuses fully to grow up, and his appeal to Olga is basically to her maternal instincts. By contrast in the scene in which Shtol'ts declares his love to her, it is she who appears to have found in Shtol'ts – not a father, but strangely enough – a mother. She confesses to believing him totally, as she would a mother (323), and, in recounting he love for Oblomov, asks Shtol'ts to bear in mind that having no mother, it was as though she were lost in a forest (324-5). This strange maternal role ascribed to Shtol'ts is reinforced when he asks her to marry him; she lays her head on his breast, 'as though on the breast of a mother' (329).

Nevertheless, Olga at first seems hostile towards Shtol'ts, at least on a subconscious level. Their proposal scene is described as a 'duel', and the military imagery is disturbingly overt. Shtol'ts is a 'dangerous enemy' and Olga realises that, if up to now she has been able 'to wage war successfully', it is not because of her own strength as 'in the struggle with Oblomov', and that 'in the open field the advantage was not on her side', therefore, by asking a parrying question: 'she merely wanted to gain an inch of ground and a moment of time, so that the enemy would disclose his plan more clearly' (321). The combative nature of Olga towards both the men she loves is here clearly expressed. It does not seem to augur well for her future marriage.

Olga at the height of her happiness, like Oblomov before her, is assailed by self doubt and apprehensiveness: 'Man is a strange creature! The more complete was her happiness, the more pensive she became, even timid' (354). Her life has reached a stage akin to Oblomovism (at least her own form of it) and she is frightened. Like Oblomov before her, she goes out into society, accompanied by Shtol'ts, but, as was the case with Oblomov, it does not produce the desired stimulus, and she hurries back to the reassuring calm of her own domestic atmosphere. She no longer wishes to keep up her correspondence with her friend Sonechka, and seems indifferent to former friends and acquaintances. She confides to Shtol'ts: 'It's as though something suddenly comes on me, some sort of depression...life seems to me... as though lacking in something.' (356)

The figure of Oblomov never seems far away from their relationship. Olga and Shtol'ts have achieved a happy life, free from passion: 'It seemed one might fall asleep and enjoy a blissful life in this well-deserved calm, as the inhabitants of quiet backwaters live in bliss.' (351) They appear to have achieved that idyll of which Oblomov, too, had dreamed (*kak mechtal i Oblomov*) (351): 'And their silence was sometimes that pensive happiness about which alone Oblomov used to dream' (351). Yet it seems to be this idyll of Oblomovism which Olga herself most fears:

She was frightened of falling into something similar to an Oblomov-like apathy. But however much she tried to rid her soul of those moments of periodic torpor, and spiritual slumber, there would gradually creep up on her – first of all a dream of happiness, a blue night would surround her and lock her in drowsiness – then a pensive period of arrest would come on, like one of life's rests – after that confusion, fear, lassitude, a sort of dull melancholy, and she would hear in her troubled head various confused vague questions. (354)

The 'blue night' is the recurrent image of her own 'Oblomovism', her own *dream* of idyllic married life. It refers to the moment in Switzerland, at the end of Part IV Chapter 4, when Shtol'ts had proposed to her: 'She still sat, for all the world as though she were asleep – so quiet was the dream of her happiness.' This quiet dream of 'happiness' has now been realised, and yet she feels that there is 'still something missing' (356) and she is aware of troubling questions. What appears to torment her is indeed a 'question', one very much to the fore in the Russia of the 1860s, yet a problem that is still a very modern one – the so-called 'female question' (*zhenskii vopros*) – the role of women in society.

At first this problem seems to be posed as one for Shtol'ts himself; he wonders how he can reconcile his active life as a man of affairs with his new domestic role (350). Yet this aspect of the problem is solved by Olga herself; she demands to take an active part in all areas of his life: 'because in a life without movement, she choked as though lacking air' (352). Not a letter, not a thought, not an action is taken without her participation, and, if Shtol'ts dares to think anything is too serious for her involvement, she scolds him for his pedantry and his cowardice (*poshlost'*), for being behind the times (*otstalost'*), calling him 'an old German periwig' (352). Nevertheless Shtol'ts himself feels that he is engaged in the process of developing his wife's potential in areas 'as yet inaccessible to the female education of the time' (352-3):

In the distance there again beckoned to him a new image, not of an egotistical Olga, not of a passionately loving wife, not of a mother-cum-nurse later fading away in a colourless, useless life, but something else, elevated, almost unheard of... (353)

It seems as though Shtol'ts has raised expectations that, for a woman, can never be realised. Although she is fulfilled as a woman with a child and a loving husband, her happy contented life no longer seems to be enough for her: '[She] demanded yet new, unheard of things, she looked further ahead.' (354) Shtol'ts has developed her intellect: 'as a thinker and an artist, he was weaving an intelligent existence for her' (353). Yet nature suggests just one thing: an endless, monotonously quiet life. She wonders whether she lacks a female heart, whether her dissatisfaction comes from the rebelliousness of a sterile mind; whether she will not become a 'blue stocking' (354). She feels that there is no one she can turn to with her problems, not even her husband, who idolises her, and in a sense has created her. When he himself raises the question of her despondency, her dismissive answer is perhaps unwittingly revealing: ' "You know what: I...am ravenously hungry!" she said, trying to laugh.' (355)

Olga's rational development, under the influence of her husband, seems to take on a religious dimension – a questioning one, typical of the 1860s:

Faith in chance happenings, the fog of hallucination disappeared from her life. A great distance, bright and free, opened up before her, and she could see, as though in translucent water, every pebble and pothole and then the clear bottom. (351)

But later, she feels that not only has she 'completed the circle of her life' in the routine life of a woman, but perhaps also there is nothing further at a more metaphysical level. Her soul keeps asking the question: 'Surely this can't be all ... all ?' (354) She fears someone might overhear this whispering of her soul and 'her eyes questioned heaven, the sea, the forest ... nowhere was there an answer: just distance, depth and darkness.' (354)

Shtol'ts attempts to reassure her that a lively and enquiring mind often attempts to penetrate beyond the boundaries of everyday life, and becomes despondent when it cannot find an answer: 'It is the sadness of the soul, questioning life about its mystery.' (357) Yet, when Shtol'ts manages to dissipate her doubts, her faith remains both in him and in God: 'But she believed in him [Shtol'ts], in a way that did not recognise any other intermediary, any authority other than God, between herself and him.' (360)

Shtol'ts chooses to address Olga's problem at a more metaphysical level rather than on the more down to earth, and more personally challenging, plane of the role of Olga as a woman. He sees it in terms of the development of the rational intellect; it is a question of maturity, he argues, a stage one passes through, when everything is clear and there are no more riddles. The despondency she feels is merely the human cost of the Promethean fire, and he associates himself with the impotence she feels: 'You and I are not Titans,' he says, 'we are not Manfreds and Fausts, prepared to struggle with recalcitrant problems ... It is not your sadness; it is the general ailment of mankind. One drop has splashed on to you.' (358) [5]   Yet, paradoxically, this is a

---

[5] Manfred and Faust are the eponymous heroes of poems by Byron and Goethe respectively.

discontentment which springs from quiet, serene happiness, as Olga confesses to Shtol'ts. 'Yes, I am unhappy perhaps through the fact that I am already too happy!' (356) The paradox is countered by paradox. Shtol'ts reassures Olga by telling her that life will not always be as easy as this. In the future it will bring losses, sadness and troubles. Listening to his words about the 'trials' *(ispytaniya)* that lie ahead, Olga's dream of the 'blue night' yields to another dream of future sorrows and tribulations. Yet amid all these trials there will be one firm point – her love for Shtol'ts. This in itself will change, because of these experiences: 'There would be no passionate sighs, no bright rays, no "blue nights", no childish romanticism: "Everything had faded and gone".' (359) The image used here for the outliving of romantic feelings is a direct reference back to an earlier stage in her emotional education – her relationship with Oblomov, who also had a dream which he obstinately refused to relinquish. But love for Olga is based, not on fleeting passions and infatuation, but on faith: 'Having once recognised in the man she had chosen his merit and his rights over her, she believed in him and therefore loved him, but should she cease to believe, she would also cease to love, as had happened with Oblomov.' (360)

Oblomov, confronted by the demands made on him by Olga, had felt an abyss open up before his feet, but Olga's strength is such that she will derive benefit from contemplating the horrors of a similar abyss; for, as Shtol'ts tells her, the doubts and fears she has 'lead to an abyss, from which you can gain nothing by questions, and they will force you to look on life with greater love ... they challenge forces already tried to a struggle with yourself, as though in order that they should not be allowed to fall asleep' (358). Shtol'ts shudders when he thinks of the life that would have awaited Olga, if she had married Oblomov. Her questions, her doubts would have ended in nothing; marriage would have been mere form without content, a framework for an everyday existence, without any aim. (361)

Shtol'ts, for his part, despite his allegiance to rationality has, through experience, come to realise the enormous power of love in human lives. He sees it as the Archimedes lever that moves the world, but, as well as truth and goodness, he is also aware that love can contain falsehood and ugliness. He has a high ideal of love, and it is obvious that he has been educating Olga towards his ideal, much as Olga had tried to do with Oblomov. But if Olga was a bright, guiding star reflected in Oblomov's stagnant waters, there is a similar sense of underfulfilment, when she herself has to measure up to Shtol'ts's ideal. Even after her crisis has passed, and Shtol'ts now realises that she is all the time growing in maturity, she still cannot measure up to his ideal: 'She grew ever taller and taller...Andrei saw that his former ideal of a woman and a wife was unattainable, but he was happy with the pale reflection of it in Olga: he had never expected even this.' (359) Yet love is not onesided: he realises that he himself must make great efforts to maintain himself as her ideal – for Olga's love is based on faith in him.

The concept of 'reflection' is also present in Oblomov's attitude to the marriage of Olga and Shtol'ts, as he himself confesses: 'I am frightened of envy; your happiness will be a mirror for me, in which I shall all the time see my own bitter and ruined (*ubitaya*) life, but, you know, I will not live any differently, I cannot' (337). Nevertheless, in spite of these pathetic words, Oblomov has, in fact, found his own happiness, and his own ideal.

Chapter VII

Agafya

If Olga can lay her head on Shtol'ts, as on a mother's breast, Oblomov himself has found another breast to turn to – one not merely to rely on, but perhaps even to 'lie' on – the breast of Agafya Matveyevna: 'high and firm as the cushion of a divan'. Oblomov is fascinated by the sly promise of these breasts; indeed the suggestion of furtive sexuality, absent from his relationship with Olga, seems to look back to his surreptitious interest in the peasant girl, who suddenly came into the description of his ideal life, as he had described it earlier to Shtol'ts.

His growing attraction to Agafya Matveyevna is seen as something quite different from the 'disease' he has just passed through – 'the small pox, measles or fever' of his love for Olga (299). Indeed, Agafya Matveyevna is presented almost as her antithesis. Her complexion is very white and seems to preclude the blush that comes so readily to Olga's face. It is stressed that she has no brows – a feature constantly remarked in the description of Olga. Olga's brows are part of her quizzical expression, and epitomise the mocking tone of her humour. The smile of Agafya Matveyevna is quite different: 'Her [ironical] smile (*usmeshka*) was more a pleasant form, by which she covered her ignorance of what to say, or what to do, in any given situation.' (235)

Oblomov's interest soon becomes transferred from Agafya Matveyevna's breasts to her bare elbows which are in constant motion. They, like the brows of Olga, seem to symbolise the woman herself – her constant work in the kitchen and about the house. The only physical work to which Olga devotes herself is the lady-like task of embroidery. The sewing of Agafya Matveyevna, by contrast, is practical and workaday; and if Oblomov fears that Olga is 'embroidering' the pattern of his life, he feels that Agafya Matveyevna is merely in danger of sewing her own nose to her skirt. (300)

Under the influence of drink, Oblomov draws a comparison between the two women for his friend Shtol'ts, and it is not to Olga's advantage. Olga, says Oblomov, can sing you 'Casta Diva', but she cannot make vodka like Agafya Matveyevna, nor can she make pies, and he rather rashly suggests that Olga might learn housekeeping from Agafya Matveyevna (339). If the language of love in Oblomov's relationship with Olga had been flowers, in his relationship with Agafya Matveyevna it is quite clearly food, and, moreover, it is she who makes the offerings. Olga had required much of Oblomov, but in his new life on the Vyborg Side it is Agafya Matveyevna who makes all the sacrifices – even to the point of pawning her jewelry and clothing in order to provide the quality of food which she knows Oblomov expects. Yet there is a social gulf between them, a barrier symbolised by the door through which in the early stages of their relationship her hand will suddenly thrust an offering of food, or through which Oblomov himself will take surreptitious glances at the twinkling, white elbows.

The way of life at Oblomovka, we had been told, was guarded like the Vestal flame (*ogon'*) passed on from generation to generation. Oblomov sees a 'flame' (*ogon'*) in Agafya Matveyevna and is increasingly attracted to its warmth; so much so that on one occasion he himself nearly catches fire (*pochti do pozhara ili po krainei mere do vspyshki*) (300). As previously with Olga he suggests that he might kiss her, to which he receives the naively serious response that it is not Holy Week.

It is clear that Oblomov has found a debased version of his ideal in this life on the Vyborg Side. As Shtol'ts says: 'It's the same old Oblomovka here, only viler' (304). Looking absent-mindedly at the face of Agafya Matveyevna, Oblomov easily confuses the present reality with his old dream of his childhood at Oblomovka. He dreams he has achieved that promised land, where the rivers flow with milk and honey, that he is cuddling up to his nurse, and that she points at Agafya Matveyevna, identifying her as the fairy-tale princess, Militrisa Kirbityevna.

This reverie is broken, as had been the earlier dream, by the advent of Shtol'ts (372), and in many respects this brief section can be seen as an updated recapitulation of the longer dream of Part I. It shows that Oblomov's new life is permeated with the values of ancient myths. The mother figure of the nurse points to another mother figure – Agafya Matveyevna – and identifies her as the ideal 'princess' of the earlier dream. As Leon Stilman has aptly observed: ' "Milk flows" – this food one does not have to earn.'[1] The importance of Spring, the period of awakening in the cycle of the year (also present behind the figure of Ilya Muromets), comes out strongly in the ritualistic nature of this life:

> Autumn, Summer and Winter passed in a languid, boring fashion, but Oblomov was waiting once more for Spring and dreamed of a trip to the country.
>
> In March they baked a whole lot of larks, in April they took out the winter frames from the windows, and declared that the Neva had opened up, and Spring had arrived. (293)

The baking of 'larks' (made in fact from dough) is, as we have seen, the indispensable ritual ensuring the benign onset of Spring in Oblomovka itself.

---

[1] See Stilman, *ibid.*, 68.

Almost from the very moment that Oblomov stepped into the house
on the Vyborg Side, we are aware of another myth echoing back from
the earlier dream. There we had been told that thunder in Oblomovka
was not terrifying, but beneficial. It came at its appointed time: 'It
almost never forgot Ilya's Day, as though to give support to that well-
known tradition among the common people' (81). The well-known folk
tradition, here referred to, is that thunder was produced by St Ilya
(Elijah) riding round heaven in his chariot. Thunderstorms could well
be expected round Ilya Day (20th July, old style), which is Oblomov's
own nameday, and the tradition is undoubtedly a pagan survival
reflecting an older superstition about the Slavonic god of thunder,
Perun, who later in Christian times became identified with St Elijah.
Thunder in Russian folklore was seen as bringing a rebirth in nature,[2]
and the figure of Ilya Muromets (whose myth, as we have seen, has
relevance for Oblomov himself) may well be equated with the dormant
power of Perun; for, in spite of his long period of quiescence, when
Ilya Muromets finally bestirred himself, he felled mighty oak trees.[3]
   When Oblomov first enters Agafya Matveyevna's house he is
impressed by the fact that it is so quiet. He asks her if she ever goes out,
and she replies that she does sometimes in summer, and quite recently
has been on an outing to the gunpowder factory on Ilya Day (233).[4]
The linking of gunpowder with Oblomov's own nameday is no mere
coincidence, as we see in the later course of the novel. It is a traditional
way of celebrating the day in the household. Nevertheless, once
Oblomov is established in the house of Agafya Matveyevna it is the 'lack
of thunder' which most seems to link his new existence with the old life
of Oblomovka:

> He looked on his present way of life as a continuation of that
> same Oblomovka existence, only with a different colouring of
> place, and, in part, of time. Here, too, as at Oblomovka he
> managed to keep life at arm's length without too much cost, make
> a bargain with it and insure himself for imperturbable peace.

[2] The renewal of the earth in Spring by thunder is evoked poetically in Mel'nikov-Pechersky's novel *In the Forests (V lesakh)*. It is an account of the folk belief of *Velik Grom Gremuchii* (a mythologised thunder) waking from his long sleep and rousing the earth (*Mat' Syra Zemlya*). See P.I. Mel'nikov (Andrei Pecherskii), *Roman v chetyrekh chastyakh*, Academia, Leningrad, 1936, Vol. 1, 441.
[3] 'One frequently encounters the confusion of Il'ya Muromets with the prophet Elijah.' Brokgauz, Efron, Vol. 24, 949. Feats similar to those of Il'ya Muromets were apparently attributed to Yeruslan Lazarevich, a figure from folk lore, with whom Oblomov also seeks to compare himself (54). See *L.P.*, 658.
[4] 'The church of Elijah the Prophet in the Gunpowder Works was built in 1784. The Gunpowder Works, established in 1715, were situated in Ochta, then a suburb of St Petersburg, not far from the Vyborg Side where Pshenitsyna lived.' Note by A.F. Zakharin in I.A. Goncharov, *Oblomov, kniga dlya chteniya s kommentariem na angliiskom yazyke*, M., 1989, 541.

He inwardly exulted that he had got away from its pestering, tormenting demands and its thunderstorms, away from that horizon beneath which the lightning of great joys flashes, and the sudden [thunder] strokes of great griefs reverberate... (367)

There is a curious irony in the fact that a hero, whose name is so clearly linked to thunder, and who celebrates his nameday at a gunpowder factory, should spend his life avoiding 'thunder' in all its metaphorical forms. Yet he himself was once capable of 'explosive' thought and action, as Shtol'ts reminds him in Part II Chapter 4 when he attempts to bring him back into the world: 'And how many wonderful fireworks came from your head!' he tells him. (143)

Now, however, Oblomov sees 'fireworks' as dangerous. After he has first blurted out his love for Olga, he thinks about the dangers of passion; he knows he would run away from a passionate woman, because: 'It's a firework, the explosion of a barrel of gunpowder; and then what? Deafness, blindness and burned hair.' (160)   Yet in introducing him to Olga, Shtol'ts had merely wanted to bring a light into his life:

...to bring a lamp into a murky room, from which an even light and several degrees of warmth would be shed into all the dark corners, and the rooms would become more happy and gay.
That was the only result he was trying to achieve in acquainting his friend with Olga. He did not foresee that he was introducing a firework, and Olga and Oblomov foresaw this even less. (175)

Yet Olga's own surname, Ilinskaya (Ilya woman), hints at the thunder and gunpowder of Ilya Day itself, and in the 'lunacy of love' which she experiences during that languidly voluptuous night in the garden, she reveals herself as the passionate woman Oblomov so fears ('the firework, the explosion of a barrel of gunpowder').   The following day, however, she has recovered, and Oblomov sends to enquire about her health.   The reply he receives is apparently reassuring, though scarcely so on a symbolic level: 'She was better, thank goodness, and he was invited to dinner, and in the evening they were all going to see the fireworks five versts away.' (212)

When later, in Part II Chapter 12, Oblomov warns Olga of the dangers of passion – the perils of the thunderstorm and the abyss – she is unimpressed, as she reflects on the whole course of their relationship, and blushingly remembers the events and non-events of that sultry night in the garden:

'You talk nothing but nonsense!' she said, quickly glancing aside, 'I have seen no lightning in your eyes at all. You look at me for the most part like...my nurse Kuzminichna!' she added and began to laugh. (220)

By contrast, Oblomov may see his own nurse figure Agafya Matveyevna as a 'flame', but she is really a fire spreading warmth, and he can safely go to the gunpowder factory with her to celebrate his nameday. Nevertheless, such visits cannot propitiate the god of thunder forever:

> In Summer they would set off out of town on Ilya Friday, to the gunpowder works, and life would flow in its usual succession, without, one could say, introducing pernicious changes, if the blows of life were never to reach these tiny, quiet corners. But unfortunately the thunder stroke, which shakes the mountains to their base and the huge expanses of the air, echoes even in the mouse-hole, though here more faintly and dimly, but it is none the less felt in the mouse-hole. (368)

The 'thunder stroke' (*gromovoi udar*) is in fact a stroke in the medical sense *(udar)* - a result, it is hinted, of the sedentary, quiet life by which Oblomov sought to avoid all 'thunder strokes' and 'fireworks'.[5] Thus the ambivalent significance of thunder for the symbolism surrounding Oblomov, and the implications of his name, can be seen as yet a further reflection of that essential ambiguity with which the hero and his values are presented throughout the novel.

Oblomov's life is as though confined in a frame of routine and ritual. This is how Shtol'ts sees the fate that would have awaited Olga, had she married Oblomov: 'Marriage would have been only form and not content, a means and not a goal: it would have served as a broad, unchanging frame for visits, the reception of guests, dinners, evenings and empty chatter ...' (361)

Nevertheless, in his life with Agafya Matveyevna this 'frame' has become golden:

> Ilya Ilich lived a life as though with a golden frame, in which there changed, as if in a diorama, only the usual phases of day and night and the seasons of the year; other changes, particularly major happenings, disturbing on the bed of life all that sediment, which is often so bitter and confused – such changes did not happen. (366)

---

5   Ehre links the numbness in Oblomov's left leg to the fairy tale told by his nurse about the bear who had lost his leg. Ehre, 178-9.

Yet, some two and a half pages later the 'golden frame' becomes the confines of the coffin:

> With the years emotions and regrets appeared less frequently, and quietly and gradually he settled into the simple and broad coffin of the remainder of his existence, one made by his own hands, as the desert fathers, who, turning from life, dig themselves a grave. (368)

Even here, it will be noted, ambivalence does not end; for in this process in which the 'golden frame' and the 'diorama' turn into the 'broad but simple coffin', the sybarite, it is suggested, has become something close to a saint.

Chapter VIII

Minor Characters

In *Oblomov* the spotlight is turned so much on the central characters that in their penumbra the outlines of less major figures often seem shadowy, less tangible. Commenting on the portrayal of Nadenka in *A Common Story*, Belinsky suggested that Goncharov's methods of characterisation might be dictated by expediency: 'As long as he needs her he takes trouble with her, and then he flings her aside.'[1]

The reader may indeed feel that at times Goncharov is merely using his characters for a given purpose, even with a figure so important for his novel as Shtol'ts. The 'Portrait Gallery' of Part I is an obvious case in point: the author seems to take care with these characters while he needs them, but then abandons them. Only Tarantyev, and to a lesser extent Alekseyev, are developed in the further course of the novel.

Another figure even more at the penumbra is Oblomov's friend Ivan Gerasimovich. In Part II Chapter 3 Oblomov gives Shtol'ts a description of his visits to Ivan Gerasimovich's quiet, comfortable apartment. It is a haven of Oblomovism with its soft divans, its plant and animal life, and its permanent supply of food. (135) Yet the reader never makes the acquaintance of Ivan Gerasimovich, never actually sees Oblomov enjoying his quiet visits there. We are told in Part II Chapter 9 that the image of Olga has banished thoughts of visiting Ivan Gerasimovich, yet by Part III Chapter 6 staying with Ivan Gerasimovich suggests itself as a solution to the problem of seeing Olga on a daily basis, given the difficulty of crossing the river from the Vyborg Side. The idea appeals to him, but Oblomovism prevents him from acting on it.

A similar shadowy confidante exists for Olga in her friend Sonechka, but she grows less and less to need Sonechka's advice – indeed her gossip about Olga and Oblomov appears to put added pressure on the relationship. Before marrying Shtol'ts she feels she would like to consult her friend on the possibility of loving more than once, but not only is Sonechka not available for such consultation, she is reputed actually to be engaged in a third love affair. (318) Once married to Shtol'ts, Olga feels no further need for her advice. She does not reply to Sonechka's letters, and consciously 'drops' her friend. (355) Even more shadowy are the figures of Olga's aunt and the

---

[1] As reported by Goncharov himself in *Luchshe pozdno, chem nikogda. Sob.soch.*, Vol. 8, 75.

'family friend' the baron (a reflection here, perhaps, of Goncharov's own mother's relationship with the more aristocratic Nikolai Tregubov?) [2]

In the penumbra surrounding the warm light of Agafya Matveyevna are her children, the servant Akulina and the even more shadowy figure of the infirm grandmother. Her brother Ivan Matveyevich Mukhoyarov is far more prominently portrayed, but he is necessary for the purposes of Goncharov's plot. Ivan Matveyevich, in collusion with Tarantyev, seeks to cheat and dupe Oblomov at every turn. First he draws up an iniquitous contract, which more or less obliges Oblomov to stay in the house on the Vyborg Side. He then persuades him to hire a corrupt bailiff, Zatertyi, who will run the estate at Oblomovka, but will be controlled by Ivan Matveyevich and Tarantyev. When Shtol'ts manages to put an end to this swindle, Ivan Matveyevich contrives to extort money from Oblomov indirectly through a supposed debt to his sister and the accompanying threat of blackmail. Shtol'ts also stops these extortionate dealings, and in so doing rids his friend of the last inimical principle threatening the outward well-being of life on the Vyborg Side: 'From the time that Shtol'ts saved Oblomovka from the thieving debts of the brother, and the brother and Tarantyev cleared off entirely, everything that was hostile also left with them from the life of Ilya Ilyich.' (366) Ivan Matveyevich and Tarantyev, therefore, have, it seems, a symbolic function in the novel: they are the hostile principle threatening the realisation of Oblomov's dream of happiness on the Vyborg Side. The threat comes from within; for Ivan Matveyevich and Tarantyev are merely the battening, black shadows of Oblomov's own inability to cope with the financial and practical bases of that life.

From the reader's first acquaintance with Mukhoyarov, it would seem that he is more of an episodic character, a middle-aged man with a 'large parcel' under his arm, glimpsed by Oblomov at the end of the street. This mysterious 'large parcel' is his *leitmotif*, the emblem of his acquisitiveness, but in this first fleeting vignette there is another indicative feature, which seems to look forward to the characterisation of Belikov in Chekhov's short story 'The Man in a Case', and the figure of Serebryakov in his play *Uncle Vanya*; for in spite of the hot, dry day Mukhoyarov is wearing rubber galoshes (236).[3]

---

[2] See Ehre, 10-13. Tregubov figures as Yakubov in Goncharov's slightly fictionalised reminiscences *Na rodine*, but here he seems also to exhibit features of proto-Oblomovism: eg his habit of lying in bed; his complete ignorance of the affairs of his estate; his shunning of contact with others (on this latter point Goncharov offers a political explanation – it stems from the fear and mistrust of other people, given the political repression after the abortive Decembrist uprising of 1825). See Goncharov, *Sob. soch.*, Vol. 7, 239-40, 242, 255-6.

[3] A.P. Chekhov, *Poln. sob.soch.*, Vol. 10, 43; Vol. 13, 66. Cf. also the description of the wily, 'buttoned up' civil servant Dobyshev in *Na rodine*. See Goncharov, *Sob. soch.*, Vol. 7, 282.

Clothing, in fact, is as indicative for his character as it is for Oblomov and Zakhar, and in the next chapter (Part III Chapter 3) we are given a more detailed description in which the secretive, 'buttoned up' nature of the man is clearly epitomised by his dress: 'His uniform was done up on all its buttons, so that it was impossible to know whether he was wearing anything [i.e. 'linen' – *bel'e*] under it or not.' (240)

Openness of character, as Lermontov had already suggested in *Hero of Our Time*, is betrayed by the movement of arms and hands whilst talking (Chekhov would later suggest as much about Lopakhin in *The Cherry Orchard*).[4] Openness such as this is obviously lacking in Mukhoyarov: 'It was as though he were ashamed of his hands, and when he spoke he would try, either to hide both of them behind his back, or one behind his back and the other in his coat breast.' (241) A single finger of one hand is as much as he is prepared to show, when explaining a document to a superior. His eyes are the most indicative of all: they have a 'double glance.' (241) They never look straight at an object at first, but alight on it only after a second glance. (240)

A little later (Part VI Chapter 1) this portrait is filled out further. We learn to our surprise that he is an epicurean in matters of food, and that although he cares nothing about his clothing, he cares about his table. Unlike Oblomov, Ivan Matveyevich does not wish his clothing to betray the essential man: 'They can't see what's in your belly, and won't go in for idle talk; whereas a heavy chain for your watch, a new frock-coat, patent-leather boots – all this gives rise to unnecessary gossip.' (294) At the same time the secret of what lies beneath the buttoned-up uniform is finally revealed – he does have underwear: 'Like a manual worker, he only changed his undergarments on Saturdays, but, as regards his table, he spared no expense.' (294)

Although the portrait of Ivan Matveyevich is rich in comic detail, and in spite of the fact that his machinations intrude substantially into Oblomov's life, he himself is far from obtrusive. Apart from certain key, set-meetings he is only perceived as a figure in the background. For the most part he is locked away in his own quarters, or merely glimpsed as that episodic figure first seen by Oblomov at the end of the street. In almost Gogolian fashion Ivan Matveyevich is reduced to a large parcel, flitting past the windows or along the outside fence. [5]

Behind Ivan Matveyevich there is an even more shadowy figure, whose characteristics are reduced to little more than a name – Zatertyi (i.e. the past participle of the verb *zateret'*, which has various connotations: 'to destroy or make something unnoticed through rubbing or smearing'; 'to squeeze or crush'; 'to purposely prevent someone getting on in a career'). It seems as though a technique of

---

4 Cf. *ibid.*, Vol. 13, 243-4 and M. Yu. Lermontov, *Sobranie sochinenii v chetyrekh tomakh*, M., 1964-5.
5 Cf. *L.P.* , 266, 240, 246, 291.

characterisation which spotlights central figures also casts a tiny shadow of mimicry behind them. For Oblomov it is Ivan Gerasimovich; for Olga – Sonechka; for Ivan Matveyevich – Zatertyi. Even for Zakhar there is Anfisa, who becomes his more efficient counterpart in Oblomov's household. For Agafya Matveyevna there is Akulina (though in the house on the Vyborg Side Anisya and Agafya Matveyevna develop an unbreakable bond, and become almost as one (294-5).

The thin, episodic characterisation of figures such as these may strike the reader as unsatisfactory; they are portrayed more as objects than as subjects in their own right, but there is perhaps a sound thematic reason for this – they are the 'others' against whom the central subject, Oblomov, has to defend the substantiality of his own ego: they cannot be allowed to intrude as real human beings.

We see this thematic 'flight from others' in the way Oblomov regards Sonechka and the tittle-tattle about his relationship with Olga, which he associates with her. Its effects, however, are most striking of all in the most developed of these minor characters, Ivan Matveyevich. It is not merely that he is first perceived by Oblomov as a man with a large parcel, and is continually reduced to this status, in spite of the greater meaning this character undoubtedly has in Oblomov's life, but his distanced 'otherness' can also be seen in the fact that he is frequently presented through a narrative device of invisible quotation marks.

Oblomov first hears about Ivan Matveyevich from his sister, and thus, through this alone, he is a character introduced at second hand. Agafya Matveyevna constantly refers to him as *bratets* ('dear little brother') and it is this term which, without any sense of direct quotation, is always used to designate him both by author and characters alike throughout the further course of the novel. Even more significantly, Agafya Matveyevna out of respect for this 'dear little brother' always refers to him in the plural (the mark of respectful humility characteristic of servants and peasants when addressing a master). It is bizarre that Agafya Matveyevna should address her own brother in this way, and the subservience it implies is strikingly at odds with the more familiar *'bratets'*, yet the dichotomy set up between 'little brother' and 'master' adds to the essential mystery of Ivan Matveyevich.

Surprisingly enough, these speech habits are adopted by Oblomov himself (initially, perhaps, ironically) when he first sees the figure with the parcel: *'Von, dolzhno-byt' i bratets prishli!'* (237) Later, however, this 'alienating' perception of Ivan Matveyevich (through the speech habits of his sister) is integrated into the narrative style itself, and is thrown into even sharper relief when, in the same sentence, the true 'master' Oblomov is referred to only in the singular:

Oblomov dined [*obedal* (sing.)] with the family at three o'clock, only the brother [*bratets*] dined [*obedali* (plur.)] apart, afterwards, mostly in the kitchen, because he arrived [*prikhodili* (plur.)] from the office very late. (295)

Ivan Matveyevich is not seen either by Oblomov, or even the narrator, in his true light; he is refracted through the consciousness of Agafya Matveyevna. As such we have a manifestation of that 'family principle' so dominant at Oblomovka, which conditioned Oblomov's own attitude to work in the civil service, and which now makes him vulnerable to one of its most rapacious representatives.

Chapter IX

Imagery

It has not been possible to discuss any aspect of the novel without reference to its imagery. Thus, as we have seen, the 'language of flowers' assumes great importance in the relationship between Oblomov and Olga. Yet of almost equal importance for Oblomov's attitude to love is the image of the 'abyss' or 'bottomless pit' (*propast'*, *bezdna*). It is a recurrent focus of fear for Oblomov, and its origins may be traced back to the ravine in Oblomovka. It is fear of the abyss (*propast'*) which makes him write his cruel letter to Olga (Part II Chapter 10) as he makes plain: 'It is only today, during this night, that I have understood how quickly my feet are slipping [from under me]. It was only yesterday that I succeeded in peering into the abyss into which I am falling, and I made up my mind to come to a halt.' (196) In the scene of reconciliation that follows, Olga mocks these fears. Oblomov's inertia, she suggests, precludes any form of movement: 'Lie on your back again, you won't make a mistake, "You will not fall into the abyss."' (203)

Perhaps the real nature of Oblomov's 'abyss' can be identified as passion. At the beginning of Part II Chapter 11, he feels himself to be nothing more than a wretched seducer: 'That's where the abyss is! and Olga does not fly above it, she is there at the very bottom.' (216) In the next chapter he tries to warn Olga of the dangers when a man gets carried away: 'Passion breathes on him, he ceases to be in control of himself ' (219). However, when towards the close of the chapter he has proposed to her, and, understanding her to have accepted him, he rushes to embrace her, Olga mockingly warns him once again of the 'abyss', linking it this time with the theme of 'thunder': 'The abyss is opening up, lightning is flashing. Be careful!' (223)

Before their final break, Olga visits him in St Petersburg, and now Oblomov declares that he is prepared to jump at once into the abyss for her, but Olga herself realises that it is already too late (274). Oblomov will not jump into any abyss, though he is, as Shtol'ts later says, in danger of falling into a pit, given the life he is leading on the Vyborg Side of the river: 'Be careful, Ilya, that you do not fall into a pit: a simple peasant woman; dirty surroundings; the suffocating ambience of stupidity; coarseness. Fie on you!' (345)

Olga, as Shtol'ts's wife, makes him promise not to desert his old friend – 'until an abyss opens up', or a wall stands between them (363). Nevertheless, on Shtol'ts's last visit to the house on the Vyborg Side, he is appalled by what he sees, and tries to drag Oblomov away with him from this pit. Oblomov refuses and points out to Shtol'ts that he is already married to Agafya Matveyevna and has a son by her. It is now that Shtol'ts feels that 'an abyss has opened up', and that there is 'a wall between them'. To Olga's anxious query about the abyss, Shtol'ts merely replies that what is happening there is 'Oblomovism' (376).

The novel's most obvious symbol is undoubtedly an item of clothing – Oblomov's *khalat*. [1] We are introduced to it at the very opening, though under the guise of a dressing gown (*shlafrok*), and we are told: 'This lack of concern was translated from his face into all the poses of his body, even into the folds of his dressing gown (*shlafrok*).'(7) Thus from the beginning this item of clothing is 'psychologised', it is an essential part of Oblomov's attitude to life. Shortly afterwards follows the more detailed description identifying the oriental nature of this garment, now designated as *khalat* rather than 'dressing gown' (*shlafrok*).(8) It is, as Oblomov later asserts, a distinguishing feature that marks him off from 'others' (77).

In Part II Shtol'ts tries to bring back the old Oblomov he knew by taking him out into St Petersburg society, but Oblomov's disillusionment and rejection of this life have their inevitable accompaniments – the *khalat* and the couch: ' "For whole days," Oblomov grumbled, putting on his *khalat*, "you don't take your boots off: your feet ache so! I don't like your St Petersburg life!" he continued lying down on the couch.' (136)

When Shtol'ts identifies Oblomov's problems as *Oblomovism* and poses the question 'now or never' Oblomov has a hard choice to make:

> This 'Oblomov question' was for him more profound than that of Hamlet. To go forward meant suddenly to throw off this broad *khalat* not only from his shoulders, but also from his soul, from his mind; and, along with the dust and the cobwebs from the walls, sweep away the cobwebs from his eyes and to see! (146)

Once he falls under Olga's spell, the symbol is rejected (148): 'Even the *khalat* seemed to him to be repulsive, Zakhar stupid and intolerable, and the dust and the cobwebs unbearable' (150).

When Oblomov, quizzing Olga on her love for him, complains that the statement 'I love' is broad enough to cover everything, Olga, as we have already seen, mischievously suggests the analogy of the *khalat*. Oblomov is so embarrassed at this barb that he even denies that he ever had such a garment (191). Olga realises that her real rival for Oblomov's affections would not necessarily be another woman. After receiving his cruel letter, she tells him this openly: 'What if it were to be not even another woman, but your *khalat,* which were dearer to you?' (202) Yet when Olga herself surrenders to doubt in Part II Chapter 11, she feels that she cannot reject her love for Oblomov, and once again the image is that of clothing: 'The deed is done; she already loved, and one cannot discard love on a whim like a dress.' (214)

---

[1] One may contrast the 'two coats' of Shtol'ts. See Ehre, 198.

The image of the dress is given more concrete expression in the next chapter, when Olga confesses that, because she and Oblomov have been at odds, she has quarrelled with her maid Katya, just as he quarrels with Zakhar, but then she tells him:

'But as soon as you arrived, I suddenly became another person. I gave Katya my lilac dress.'
'That's love!' he pronounced with emotion.
'What? A lilac dress?' (217)

Although the dress is 'lilac' (*lilovoe*) it is not the same word as the symbolic blossom (*siren'*). Nevertheless, Oblomov's unexpected identification of it with 'love' clearly underlines the symbolic nature of the gesture.

During the idyllic summer at the *dacha* the *khalat* has entirely disappeared from Oblomov's life. Tarantyev has taken it along with his other things to the house on the Vyborg Side of the river. (148) Yet this in itself is an omen for its future ascendancy. In the autumn, when Oblomov first settles there, he is still under Olga's influence ('He had long ago said farewell to his *khalat* and had given orders that it be hidden in a cupboard') (238), but it is found and admired by Agafya Matveyevna who promises to wash and mend it for him, because, as she says, there is still a lot of wear (i.e. 'service') in it. Then, once again, Oblomov's love and his *khalat* become linked through Agafya Matveyevna's remark that he will be able to put this garment on before his wedding. However, on this occasion, Oblomov's embarrassment stands in ironic contrast to his earlier quizzing of Olga on her 'love'; for Oblomov's resulting confusion now stems not from the *khalat,* but from mention of the word 'marriage'. (264) The proposed marriage is, in fact, a great embarrassment to him, and in the end it is the *khalat* which wins out. After his final break with Olga, Oblomov is emotionally shattered, and as if to underline that the loss is irrevocable, Zakhar performs a highly symbolic act:

Ilya Ilich scarcely noticed Zakhar taking off his clothes, pulling off his boots and throwing on his shoulders – the *khalat*!
'What is that?' he merely asked, looking at the *khalat*.
'The landlady brought it this morning: the *khalat* has been washed and mended,' said Zakhar. (290)

From this point on Oblomov wears his *khalat* under the watchful eye of Agafya Matveyevna, and in Part IV Chapter 1 he is so impressed by her concern for his *khalat* that he makes a suggestion he had wanted to make to Olga – that they should go and live on his estate. (301)

It is obvious that the condition of the *khalat* mirrors the state of Oblomov's fortunes, and by Chapter 5 of Part IV things have taken a different turn: Oblomov has been blackmailed into paying money over to Agafya Matveyevna's brother and Tarantyev. Oblomov and Agafya Matveyevna can hardly make ends meet, and we read: 'The *khalat* on Oblomov was worn out, and however carefully the holes in it were sewn up, it was falling apart everywhere and not just at the seams: a new one had been needed long ago.' (330)

When, in the next chapter, Shtol'ts visits Oblomov, he is appalled at the state of squalor that everything appears to be in, and he calls special attention to the *khalat*, telling Oblomov he should throw it away. Oblomov, of course, cannot bring himself to do so: 'Habit, Andrei; I can't bear to part with it,' he says (335). By Chapter 9 Shtol'ts has sorted out Oblomov's financial problems, and life in the house on the Vyborg Side is now full of peace and contentment, so much so that Agafya Matveyevna, symbolically, is again working away to restore the *khalat*. Oblomov lying on his couch watches her quickly moving elbows and, as used to happen at Oblomovka, he keeps nodding off to the comforting sounds of women sewing. (365)

Throughout his life Oblomov needs the reassuring support of active women, yet there is something markedly feminine in his own character. This is suggested from the outset in the physical description of him given on the opening page of the novel: 'In general, judging by the dull, excessively white coloration of his neck, his small, puffy hands, the lack of firmness of his shoulders, his body seemed too pampered for that of a man.' (7)

In Part II Chapter 10 after Oblomov's cruel letter to Olga, reconciliation and a new stage in their relationship appear to have taken place. Nevertheless, as Olga's comments make plain, Oblomov is still assuming the feminine role:

> 'Now I am not afraid!' he said cheerfully. 'With you fate is not terrifying!'
> 'I have read these words not long ago, in Sue, I think,' she objected, turning towards him with sudden irony, 'only there it was a woman who said them to a man.'
> The colour rushed to Oblomov's face. (204)

Later, as we have seen, she will accuse him of looking at her, not with the eyes of passion, but with an expression that reminds her of her old nurse.

The summer draws on and Oblomov still seems incapable of taking those practical steps to arrange his affairs, which Olga has stipulated as a precondition of their official betrothal. Until this happens, she says, their meetings must be few and discreet. Oblomov is pleased to lose even this 'organisational' burden: ' "Yes, that is true," he said, happy that she had taken on the care of deciding when they should meet.' (238) Given this abrogation of responsibility, it is not surprising that he now finds difficulty in visiting Olga, and it is she who, quite unconventionally, decides to call on him in his apartment on the Vyborg Side of the river. This reversal of socially accepted sexual roles exhilarates him. Yet, strangely, as he triumphantly recalls the words of Olga herself, there seems to be hope for his own masculinity:

> 'Forward! Forward!' Olga said, 'Higher and higher on to that boundary where tenderness and grace lose their powers, and where the kingdom of the male begins.' (276)

Although he now thinks of himself as 'her leader and guide', the mood is short-lived; significantly, a mere article of clothing can cause him to reject her. She has left her glove behind, and in Oblomov's mind this soon turns from a lover's token, a pledge of her hand, into a cause for acute personal embarrassment, once it has been noticed and commented on by others.

Ambiguity in the sexual role, however, is not confined to Oblomov alone. It is obvious that in her relations with him Olga herself is forced into more masculine attitudes and behaviour, but her doubts only become explicit in her marriage to Shtol'ts, when her own moment of 'Oblomovism' in Part IV Chapter 8 leads her to question her very nature:

> She knew whom she could ask about these anxieties, and she would have found an answer, but what kind of an answer? What if this were the protest of an untalented mind, or, still worse, the thirst of an unfeminine heart, not created for sympathy! (354)

For his part Shtol'ts, too, feels under pressure from Olga in his masculine role:

> At the same time, almost all his life, he had to face the not inconsiderable concern of maintaining his male prestige at the same level, in the eyes of a self-respecting and proud Olga, not from trivial jealousy, but so that this pure crystal life should not be clouded, and this might happen if her faith in him were in the slightest shaken. (360)

A recurrent image throughout the novel is the river as a symbol for life.[2] Its origin, like much else, is to be found in 'The Dream'. For the inhabitants of Oblomovka life is a river, and they are merely the spectators of its flow:

---

[2] Ehre also discusses the 'river' imagery. *Ibid.*, 175, 181.

Life like a quiet river flowed past them, and all that remained for them was to sit on the bank of that river and watch the inevitable events which presented themselves, uncalled for, to every one in turn. (97)

In the latter part of the novel 'the river', both as image and reality, begins to assume an important role. Oblomov is now separated from Olga and from the life of the capital city by the river Neva. The last effort he makes to see Olga before the onset of winter becomes, at her suggestion, a boat trip on the autumnal river. Throughout the whole course of this meeting Oblomov seems unhappy and ill at ease. He had sensed the coming of winter in the bare, leafless trees and the noisy cawing of the crows, and now he has cold river water splashed in his face by a playful Olga (he who as a child was protected from the snow, and who felt the cold on the first of May). Once he is safely back on the Vyborg Side, doubts again assail him, and he is not reassured by the 'river' of life:

With loud sighs he would lie down, or get up, he even went out on to the street, and all the time he was searching for a norm of life, the sort of existence which would be filled with content, and would flow quietly, day after day, drop by drop, in the silent contemplation of nature and those quiet, scarcely moving events of a peacefully busy family life. He could not bring himself to imagine life as a broad river noisily rushing along, with seething waves, as Shtol'ts imagined it to be. 'That is like a disease,' said Oblomov, 'fever, racing along over rapids, bursting through dams, flooding.' (264-5)

Soon, however, because of the wintry conditions, the pontoon bridges have to be seasonally removed from the Neva. Oblomov now has the river itself as an excuse for not visiting Olga, so that, if the river is to be taken as symbolic of life, it would now seem that life itself has come between them. Once the bridges are reestablished, it is Olga who makes the crossing to visit Oblomov. When she has gone, Oblomov experiences a short-lived state of euphoria in which it seems the flow of life has once more been vindicated in the confluence of two life-streams: 'Both lives, like two rivers, must merge together: he was her guide and leader!' (276) In reality, of course, an actual river still lies between them separating his life from hers.

Yet Shtol'ts has his own view of life as a river:

He would not have wanted turbulent passion, as neither did Oblomov, only for different reasons. He would, however, have liked his feelings to flow along an even course, after seething passionately at their source, in order to drink and assuage himself, and then all his life know the source of this spring of happiness. (316)

It is Shtol'ts who offers Olga the real river of life – the impressive flow with spacious views. It is Shtol'ts who has:

...given his hand and led her out, not into the glare of blinding rays, but as though on to the full flow of a broad river, with vast fields and friendly smiling hills ... With quiet joy her glance found calm in the full flow of life, its broad fields and green hills. (329-30)

This, as it were, is married life in perspective. In marriage itself Shtol'ts finds that he has to provide 'a smooth flow of life' (*davat' plavnoe techenie zhizni*) (351) but his attention has only to lapse for 'life to well up like a spring' once more for Olga (*zhizn' bila klyuchom*) (351) and it is as though she begins to see the perspectives of the 'river of life' too clearly: 'She could see, as though in translucent water, every pebble and pothole and then the clear bottom.' (351)

By contrast Oblomov has found his own placid stream in the 'golden frame of life' on the Vyborg Side of the river and its slow flow and clarity is a source of comfort, without those changes which disturb the sediment from 'the bed of life' (366).

Yet change, of course, there is for the inhabitants of the Vyborg Side of the river – change which is constantly seen in geological terms, as the slow flattening of their domestic landscape:

[Life] was changing all the time in its various forms, but the change was that slow gradual one with which the geological transformations of our planet take place. There a mountain gradually crumbles, here the sea for whole centuries brings mud or retreats from the shore yielding an increase of soil. (292)

Such geological change, we are told, takes place in the relationship of Anisya to Agafya Matveyevna herself (though here the gradual silting of the sea, the crumbling of mountains, are also accompanied by slight volcanic emissions) (294-5). The end of a geological era also comes in a natural, if more dramatic way with the thunder clap, that shakes the bases of the mountains, but, as Goncharov makes plain, is also felt in the mousehole. The silting up of Oblomov's life has led to a stroke.

Chapter X

Conclusion

From our examination of the novel we can see that *Oblomov* is not only rich in themes and imagery, but that for all its apparent looseness of form, it is, nevertheless, a coherent and well-constructed work of art. On finishing the bulk of the novel in 1857, Goncharov wrote:

> I saw that in my work it was not a matter of the style but of the fullness and the completed quality of the whole edifice. It appeared to me as though it were a whole city and that the reader had been so placed that he could view it all and see whether the suburbs were consonant with the whole, how the towers and parks were disposed, but not to penetrate down to such detail as [to see] whether the material used were stone or brick, whether the roofs were smoothly even, the windows decorated with figures etc. etc.[1]

Nevertheless the reader who does interest himself in Goncharov's building blocks and the fineness of his detail will still be impressed by the architect's striving for organic coherence. We have already seen that the narrative technique echoes the central theme of passivity in as much as Goncharov, in telling his tale, frequently presents his reader with states resulting from the character's actions rather than the actions themselves, and that such congruity of form and content extends to the language itself. Thus the argument about 'love' in Part II Chapter 9 is centred on the difference between active and passive verbal forms of the concept: *ya lyublu* as opposed to *ya vlyublen*. The one dramatic action that our passive hero undertakes is to slap Tarantyev's face when he goes too far in his vilification of Shtol'ts and Olga. Yet, significantly, here the author chooses the passive voice to convey such uncharacteristic violence:

> A loud slap resounded in the room. Tarantyev, struck by Oblomov on the cheek, instantly fell silent, sank down on to a chair and rolled his stupefied eyes around in amazement. (346)

Such choice of grammatical form is not fortuitous.

The heartland of passivity is Oblomovka itself. There all action stands still, and the temporal stasis of Oblomovka is reflected in the language used to describe it, as D.S. Likhachev has observed:

---

[1] Geiro, *L.P.*, 574.

In Oblomovka there is nothing sudden, nothing which does not take place according to the calendar...Grammatical forms and aspects are joined together in a single phrase: transitions from the past tense to the present and from the future to the past underline the fact that time in Oblomovka has no special significance. [2]

The 'grammatical aspects' to which Likhachev here refers are the aspects of the Russian verb – imperfective and perfective – a duality in the perception of action, which is of prime importance in the structure of the language itself. In crude terms the imperfective conveys the concept of action in its very process, whereas the perfective can view action in its completion (i.e. as an achieved state).

Thus to develop Likhachev's point, by stressing Goncharov's use of aspect rather than tense, it seems significant that in the 'Dream of Oblomov' the author often chooses to convey even the repeated actions of habit through the perfective future, rather than the imperfective past, and that even his depiction of the recurrent ritual in Oblomovka is projected through a series of infinitives in the perfective aspect: the very habits and rituals of Oblomovka have more the quality of an achieved state.[3] It also seems significant that the perfective aspect is chosen to convey those heavily symbolic statements about the fading of lilacs (*poblekli, pobleknut, otoshli*) – again it is *state* rather than *action* which is at issue.

But the matter goes deeper than this: the duality represented by Oblomov and Shtol'ts reflects the duality of action as it is conceptually perceived in Russian through its aspectual system. The *perfective* is the aspect of Oblomov – the embodiment of the achieved state; the possibility of action only in the past or the future: the *imperfective* is the aspect of Shtol'ts – action in progress; action in the present; habitual and constant action both in the past and the future.[4]

Life for Shtol'ts is continual process: 'Labour is the form, content, basic element and aim of life, at least of mine,' (144) he tells Oblomov, and at the end of Chapter 2 Part IV he makes a significant admission: 'Bear in mind that life itself and labour are the aim of life, and not a woman.' (306)   This refusal to see a woman as an aim in life helps to

---

[2] Quoted in Kantor, 162.

[3] Cf. ' После чая все займутся чем-нибудь: кто пойдет к речке и тихо бродит по берегу, толкая ногой камешки в воду; другой сядет к окну и ловит глазами каждое мимолетное явление: пробежит ли кошка по двору, пролетит ли галка, наблюдатель и ту, и другую преследует взглядом и кончиком своего носа ... ' (91)

'Кого где посадить, что и как подать, кто с кем уехать в церемонии, примету ли соблюсти - во всем этом никто никогда не делал ни малейшей ошибки в Обломовке.' 97)

[4] The tenses of the imperfective aspect are: present, imperfective past, imperfective future. The perfective aspect has no present tense; for although the form exists it has a future meaning. On the other hand, the past tense of the perfective aspect may often have a present tense (i.e. 'perfect').

explain why he and Olga experience such difficulties in marriage as a 'state'. Disappointment in love is quite different for Oblomov: 'But I thought that [love] would hang over lovers like a sultry midday and nothing would move, or breathe in its atmosphere. But there is no peace in love; it's always moving somewhere on and ahead ... "like the whole of life", Shtol'ts says, and the Joshua has not yet been born who might say to it: "Halt! Do not move!"'(207)   Indeed, it is apparent that Shtol'ts, for his part, can only see such 'states' as sorrow and happiness in terms of actions: 'It seemed as though he controlled even sorrows and joys like the movements of his arms, like the steps he took with his feet, or as he dealt with good or bad weather.' (128)

The argument on Oblomovism in Part II Chapter 4 goes to the heart of the matter. Oblomov's perception of the ideal life is 'perfective', and when Shtol'ts dismisses this ideal as 'Oblomovism', Oblomov counter-attacks in words which suggest a much broader target than Shtol'ts himself:

> 'Where then is the ideal of life, according to you? How is it different from *Oblomovism?*' he asked, gently and dispassionately. 'Is not everybody trying to achieve the same thing that I dream of? Goodness gracious!' he added more boldly, 'surely the aim of all your running around, passions, wars, trade and politics is the striving towards this ideal of a lost paradise?' (142)

At a philosophical level the tension between these two aspects of perception, the imperfective (*nesovershennyi*) and the perfective (*sovershennyi*) leads to an argument on the nature of perfection (*sovershenstvo*) in life. Yet Oblomov's ideal of perfection is either in the past ('a lost paradise') or in the future ('the thing he dreams of') – the present seems a blank; hence his repeated cry 'When can one begin to live?'

Shtol'ts's ideal may appear to be in the future, but it is actually rooted in the present, not in achievement itself, but in the process of achieving. As Dostoyevsky's 'underground man' would later say, in his comparison of man to a chess player, who only likes the process of achieving the goal and not the goal itself:

> And who knows (one cannot guarantee it) perhaps the whole goal on earth towards which humanity is striving only consists in the mere continuity of the process of achievement, in other words, in life itself and not actually in the goal, which, of course, can only be nothing more than twice two equals four, that is a formula.

But, you know, twice two equals four is no longer life, Gentlemen, but the beginning of death. [5]

Jane Ellen Harrison first identified the two central male characters of Goncharov's novel with the aspects of the Russian verb, but her interpretation is the inverse of the one offered above. Thus she saw Shtol'ts as 'the perfective incarnate, he is for getting a thing put through' (and this in spite of the fact that earlier she had stated: 'Abstraction then rather than achievement is, if I am right, from the outset the very pith and marrow of the perfective').[6]

Paradoxically, Jane Harrison's argument may also have right on its side; for at first glance Shtol'ts does represent 'achievement' and Oblomov – 'non-achievement'. The fact that two contrary views may be accommodated within the grammar of aspect is not entirely unexpected, given the fact that it is a system entirely predicated on a dualistic perception of action, and as such ambivalence and ambiguity are of its essence. The problem is further compounded by the author's own tendency (noted in Chapter I) to view 'actions' as 'states' - a tendency which conditions his narrative procedures as well as his apparent reluctance to portray the activities of Shtol'ts.

Moreover, if Dostoyevsky's underground man is right in his formulation of the 'imperfective' nature of man, one has then to ask who it is who is really concerned with the imperfective process which he identifies as 'life itself '? Is it Shtol'ts who doubts the possibility of ever attaining his aim in life (130), or is it Oblomov who has to settle for an imperfect realisation of his ideal? In different senses, of course, it is both. Equally, but in different ways, both are denied ultimate achievement, and just as the aspects of the Russian verb bear a contradictory but symbiotic relationship to one another, the symbiosis which binds Oblomov and Shtol'ts is also complicated and far from unambiguous.[7]

Goncharov's principal concern in his masterpiece *Oblomov* may well have been to write a love story. Indeed, in all his novels the analysis of love is his chief preoccupation, and it is significant that in his article on Griboyedov's classic comedy *Woe from Wit* ('A Million Torments') (1872) it is unrequited love which Goncharov singles out as

---

[5] F.M. Dostoyevsky, *Polnoe sobranie sochinenii v tridtsati tomakh*, L., 1972-, Vol. 5, 118-19.

[6] Jane Ellen Harrison, *Aspects, Aorists and the Classical Tripos*, Cambridge, 1919, 18, 29.

[7] Ehre, for example, argues that the 'discrete particularity' of the allegorical opposition of Oblomov and Shtol'ts is ultimately overcome, and points to a further paradox: 'It is certainly the most perplexing aspect of the novel that Oblomov in his apparent spiritual defeat seems very much alive and real while Shtol'ts in his success is a lifeless abstraction.' See Ehre, 201, 219.

the force motivating the hero's actions and statements – not social conscience: the view of more conventional critics.[8]

Nevertheless his own novel about love, *Oblomov*, has an obvious social dimension, and it is this, together with the sense that it is also a parable of both national and general human significance, that lifts it above its companion novels. His hero may fail the demanding test of a challenging love, but he is still a man of the heart. The eulogy pronounced on Oblomov towards the end of the novel by his friend Shtol'ts is in effect a panegyric to his heart. The praise is fulsome and exaggerated, and there are moments, particularly in most of the English translations, that test the credulity of the reader. Thus we are told in the Magarshack translation: 'His heart cannot be bribed; he can be relied on always and anywhere.' (459) Of course, as Shtol'ts and Olga know from bitter experience, Oblomov himself cannot be relied on – except to let them down. The correct pronoun here would be 'it' not 'he'; for it is the essential soundness of Oblomov's *heart* that Shtol'ts is at pains to stress.

We have seen how Oblomov's 'heart', his concern for human values, can rouse him from lethargy to confront the callous, fashionable views of Penkin, and that the virtue of his heart captivates both Olga and Agafya Matveyevna, yet there is much in Oblomov's conduct which seems to belie the laudatory words of his friend. The praise of Oblomov's heart has much to do with the parabolic element which the novel contains. Oblomov is 'the Russian', his antithesis in the novel is Shtol'ts, the embodiment of western values. The Russian may not as yet rise to the challenge of these values, but he has much himself to offer: to the rationality and efficiency of Shtol'ts are opposed the inchoate virtues of the broad Russian heart. This heart is more than once referred to as 'gold', yet it is treasure which is deeply buried: gold covered by all kinds of dross. Like the Dostoyevskian 'broad Russian soul' (*The Brothers Karamazov*) Oblomov's broad Russian heart is full of laceration of the self and torment for others, but there is hope of resurrection, as there is for Dostoyevsky's heroes; or again, as in folk-lore, Ilya Ilyich, like Ilya of Muromets, may suddenly rise from his lethargy to perform doughty deeds. This does not happen in the novel, but the suggested resolution is not unlike that found at the end of *The Brothers Karamazov:* Russia's future lies with the younger generation.[9] Oblomov's son, like his father, is wholly Russian, but he bears the Christian name of Shtol'ts, and will be brought up by Shtol'ts and Olga to be the Oblomov of the future. The parable suggests that the great potential may yet be realised – in the future, at least.

---

8 Goncharov, *Sob. soch.*, Vol. 8, 7-40.
9 F.M. Dostoyevsky, *Poln. sob. soch.*, Vol. 14, 100; Vol. 15, 189-96.

SELECT BIBLIOGRAPHY
Texts of the Novel

Goncharov, I.A., *Oblomov, Roman v chetyrekh chastyakh*, ed. L.S. Geiro, L., 1987.

Goncharov, I.A., *Sobranie sochinenii v vos'mi tomakh*, M., 1952-5.

Goncharov, I.A., *Oblomov, kniga dlya chteniya s kommentariem na angliiskom yazyke*, M., 1989.

Goncharov, Ivan, *Oblomov*, Translated and with an Introduction by David Magarshack, Harmondsworth, 1959.

Critical Works

Baratoff, Natalie, *Oblomov, A Jungian Approach: A Literary Image of the Mother Complex*, Bern - Frankfurt am Main – New York – Paris, 1990.

Blot, Jean, *Ivan Gontcharoff ou le Réalisme Impossible*, Saint-Amand (Cher), 1986.

Chemena, O.M., *Sozdanie dvukh romanov: Goncharov i shestidesyatnitsa E.P. Maikova*, M., 1966.

Dobrolyubov, N.A., 'Chto takoe Oblomovshchina?' *Sobranie sochinenii v devyati tomakh*, M.-L., 1961-4, Vol. 4, 307-44.

Dobrolyubov, N.A., 'What is Oblomovschina?' *Selected Philosophical Essays* (trans. J.Fineberg), Foreign Languages Publishing House, M., 1956, 174-217.

Druzhinin, A.V., *Oblomov*. Roman I.A. Goncharova. Dva toma, Spb., 1895, *Biblioteka dlya chteniya*, 1895, No.12, otd. IV, 1-25. (Also in Druzhinin, A.V., *Prekrasnoe i vechnoe*, M., 1988, 441-61.

Ehre, Milton, *Oblomov and his Creator: The Life and Art of Ivan Goncharov*, Princeton, New Jersey, 1973.

I.A. Goncharov v russkoi kritike: sbornik statei (vstupitel'naya stat'ya M. Ya. Polyakova; primechaniya S.A. Trubnikova), M., 1958.

Kantor, V., 'Dolgii navyk k snu' (Razmyshleniya o romane I.A. Goncharova *Oblomov*), *Voprosy literatury*, No.1, 1989, 149-85.

Loshchits, Yu., *Goncharov (Zhizn' zamechatel'nykh lyudei)*, M., 1977.

Lyngstad, Alexandra and Sverre, *Ivan Goncharov*, New York, 1971.

Mel'nik, V.I., 'Filosofskie motivy v romane A.A. Goncharova *Oblomov* (k voprosu o sootnoshenii "sotsial'nogo" i "nravstennogo" v romane)', *Russkaya literatura*, 1982, No.3, 81-99.

Mel'nik, V.I., *Realizm I.A. Goncharova*, Vladivostok, 1985.

Setchkarev, Vsevolod, *Ivan Goncharov: His Life and Works*, Würzburg, 1974.

Stilman, Leon, 'Oblomovka Revisited', *American Slavic and East European Review*, Vol. VII, 1948, 45-7.

Tseitlin, A.G., *I.A. Goncharov*, M., 1950.

Zakharkin, A.F., *Roman I.A. Goncharova 'Oblomov'*, M., 1963.

Other Sources

Brokgauz, F.A. and I.A. Efron (eds), *Entsiklopedicheskii slovar'*, St Petersburg, 1895.

Chekhov, A.P., *Polnoe sobranie sochinenii i pisem v tridsati tomakh*, M., 1974-83.

Dostoevskii, F.M., *Polnoe sobranie sochinenii v tridtsati tomakh*, L., 1972 - .

Freeborn, Richard, *The Rise of the Russian Novel: Studies in the Russian Novel from 'Eugene Onegin' to 'War and Peace'*, London, Cambridge, 1973.

Gifford, Henry, *The Novel in Russia: From Pushkin to Pasternak*, London, 1964.

Gogol, N.V., *Polnoe sobranie sochinenii* (Akademiya nauk SSSR, L., 1937-52).

Harrison, Jane Ellen, *Aspects, Aorists and the Classical Tripos*, Cambridge, 1919.

Katarskii, I., *Dikkens v Rossii: Seredina XIX veka*, M., 1966.

Lermontov, M. Yu., *Sobranie sochinenii v chetyrekh tomakh*, M., 1964-5.

Mel'nikov, P.I. (Andrei Pecherskii), *V Lesakh: Roman v chetyrekh chastyakh*, Academia, L., 1936.

Peace, R.A., *The Enigma of Gogol: An Examination of the Writings of N.V. Gogol and their Place in the Russian Literary Tradition*, Cambridge, 1981.

Rybakov, B.A., *Yazychestvo drevnei Rusi*, M., 1987.

Walicki, A., *The Slavophile Controversy: History of a Conservative Utopia in Nineteenth Century Thought* (trans. Hilda Andrews-Rusiecka), Oxford, 1975.